Manual for Massage Therapy Educators

with a Special Section for Massage School Owners and Administrators

Laura Allen and Ryan Hoyme

**The forms in this book are available to download so you may customize them to fit your school or classroom.
E-mail a copy of your receipt to Massagenerd@gmail.com
to receive your download**

Copyright 2012 Allen & Hoyme Publishing

ISBN-13: 978-0615667287

ISBN-10: 0615667287

DEDICATION

For all the teachers, and the students, who have helped
me along me way
~ Laura Allen

In memory of my sister, Beth Hoyme
June 5, 1981 – April 12, 1999

and in appreciation of my parents, my wife Yvette,
and my daughters Alexa and Bea for all their support
through the years
~Ryan Hoyme

Acknowledgements

We would like to acknowledge Jan Schwartz for her invaluable advice in the development of this book. Thank you also to the educators who contributed tips for effective teaching: Mukti Michael Buck, Gloria Coppola, Taya Countryman, Karen Curran, Scott Dartnall, Earon Human Davis, Susie Davis, Xerlan Deery, Shauna Flagg, Barry Green, Karen Hobson, Lee Kalpin, Craig Knowles, David Lauterstein, Alexei Levine, Kenny Lyons, Lisa A. Mellers, Patricia J. Pape, Lisa Santorini, Gail Sebie, Ivy Jo Staton, Jan Schwartz, Brian TeWater, Ariana Vincent, and Tracy Walton. Thank you to our families, who have sometimes taken the backseat to our work without complaint. We thank the many teachers we have had over the years, and also owe a huge debt of gratitude to the students we have taught; they have given us our own education.

Preface

This book is primarily meant to help the owners and administrators of privately owned, independent massage schools, and teachers everywhere, both entry-level instructors and continuing education providers. Please remember that this book is meant to be general practical advice, and is not meant to replace any legislative mandates that may be in place in your state. For those who work for corporate-owned chains, you may find some of the information in this book helpful, but we don't expect anyone to break company policies and procedures that are already in place for your institution.

We are offering plain and simple advice for the management of your school and your classroom, based on our combined years of experience as massage therapists working in massage school administration, instructing in massage schools, providing continuing education, acting as consultants to the profession, and self-employed entrepreneurs.

The landscape of massage education is changing at a rapid pace. Technology has made distance education a common thing. Corporate career school chains have taken the place of many of the "mom and pop" schools that were common ten or fifteen years ago. Stricter rules and government budget cuts have left private schools lacking certain qualifications stripped of the ability to offer financial aid. Just like the lone massage therapist who is trying to make a living, massage schools are struggling to survive.

There are only a few states left in the US without massage therapy regulation. There is currently no uniform, nation-wide standard for teachers, or schools, any more than there is a nation-wide regulation or complete portability for massage therapists. The Federation of State Massage Therapy Boards, which currently has about 45 member Boards, is working towards portability by encouraging all states to adopt their Massage & Bodywork Licensing Exam (MBLEx) exclusively and by creating a Model Practice Act, but the wheels of legislation turn very slowly—and that's 45 states with different laws governing massage therapy. Attaining total portability can be compared with airplane travel to one of those galaxies beyond our own, at the far ends of the universe...we may get there sometime, but not with what we have to work with right now.

There is a huge variance in what state boards require of massage schools, and the degree to which they spell that out. Any advice that we offer here is not meant to replace any rules, laws, or requirements of your state board. It's your personal obligation to know—and follow—the letter of the law.

While the National Certification Board of Therapeutic Massage & Bodywork is still widely accepted as the go-to approval body for providers of continuing education, some states impose their own application process and rules on CE instructors. As this book is being written, the Federation of State Massage Therapy Boards is working on an initiative to start approving providers of continuing education, as well. As of press time, the NCBTMB is also doing a major overhaul of their own approval program, returning to vetting the individual classes as they used to do when they first started, instead of just approving providers. They expect to have the CE approval process completely online by late 2012. They are also in the process of bringing forth a new credentialing process and updated requirements for National Certification, including an increase from 500 to 750 hours of education, keeping current CPR certification, and submitting to a criminal background check, among other things.

The Alliance for Massage Therapy Education is a young organization for educators, massage schools, and continuing education providers. The AFMTE has undertaken a project to define teacher standards, both entry-level and advanced. Begun in 2011, they estimate the project will take between five and ten years to be refined. This work in progress will spell out the knowledge, skills, and attributes necessary for effective teaching. While the Alliance is not a regulatory organization, we expect the standards will have a significant impact on the state of education. The Alliance has an ongoing mission of getting massage more recognized and integrated into the mainstream health care delivery system. We are both active members of this organization, and encourage all educators to join. The Alliance also seeks industry partners.

COMTA, the Commission on Massage Therapy Accreditation, has accredited less than 100 massage schools and/or programs in their 10+ years of existence. While there are a number of career school accrediting bodies that accredit everything from airline pilot schools to locksmith training programs, COMTA is the only entity devoted specifically to massage and Asian bodywork programs, although they recently also began to approve esthetician programs. The accreditation process is a thorough process of self-examination for a massage program, and a deliberate act of voluntarily meeting standards of educational excellence. COMTA accredited schools are allowed to participate in Title IV funding, reason enough in itself to seek the accreditation.

In the past couple of years, the Massage Therapy Body of Knowledge (MTBOK) project was undertaken as a joint effort between the professional organizations representing massage therapy. The purpose of the project was to define the skills and knowledge of an entry-level massage therapist, something else that has been lacking in our field. It is a living, evolving document that has been opened several times for public comment. It's not perfect—according to some—and of course, you can't please all of the people all of the time. The Alliance for Massage Therapy Education is also working on a line-by-line review of the document, as we go to press.

All of these things—and more—seem to be happening at once, and the massage profession is having some growing pains. We're in that state of limbo between being a trade and being a profession, but we're moving forward every day—or almost every day. Unfortunately, legislation still pops up from time to time that is detrimental to massage therapists. Both the American Massage Therapy Association and Associated Bodywork & Massage Professionals keep legislative updates posted on their respective websites. It's wise for school owners and educators to keep informed of legislation; it can affect you and your students at any time.

In order for schools to remain profitable in a changing market, diligence in management has to be a hallmark. Excellence in teaching has to be a hallmark. Unless you're the only game in town, there's stiff competition for education dollars. The same goes for CE providers...in some places, there seems to be one on every corner. People seeking continuing education are often looking for the closest thing, the most convenient thing (hence the meteorically rising segment of distance learning) or the cheapest thing, sometimes without regard for whether it even holds interest for them or not.

We hope you will gain some valuable insight from this book, and find useful the tools we offer to help you along the way. We have included a lot of customizable forms for school and classroom management, in addition to offering practical advice that we've gleaned from our own years of working in the massage therapy education environment. If you're just starting out as a teacher or as a school owner, or if you've been struggling and hoping to turn things around, we hope you'll find it helpful.

Laura Allen and Ryan Hoyme

From the Authors, About the Authors

LauraAllenMT

For over 20 years, I was a chef and restaurant owner. I was tired of that career and looking for something else to do that didn't require me to work 90 hours a week when I took a job as the registrar of a massage school. The second day I was there, the owner said "Great! You can teach marketing." I looked at her like she was crazy and told her I'd never taken a marketing class in my life, and she said "But you've had a successful service-based business for over 20 years, and that's what being successful in the massage profession is all about—giving good service."

A couple of days after that, I enrolled in a weekend program at the school. I also had a degree in psychology, and three years of experience teaching in the public school system. I ended up teaching marketing and professional ethics to my own class while I was in school and I've been teaching in the massage field ever since. I was promoted to school administrator, and stayed in that position for five years before leaving to open my own practice, where I employ a chiropractor, an acupuncturist, aesthetician, and a half-dozen massage therapists.

For the past decade, I've been a provider of continuing education, a consultant to massage schools, other CE providers and massage therapists. I am the author of three massage-related books: *Plain & Simple Guide to Therapeutic Massage & Bodywork Examinations* (2nd ed., LWW, 2010); *One Year to a Successful Massage Therapy Practice* (LWW, 2008), and *A Massage Therapist's Guide to Business* (LWW, 2011). I am a regular contributor to trade journals. Since 2007, I have been blogging, usually about legislation and regulation in the massage profession. My blog is featured as *The Massage Pundit* at www.massagemag.com, as part of the *Women in Bodywork Business* blog at www.massagetoday.com, and is also featured on the www.massageprofessionals.com website.

I'm a founding member of the Alliance for Massage Therapy Education, a past delegate to the Federation of State Massage Therapy Boards, served for five years on the North Carolina Board of Massage & Bodywork Therapy, am a current member of the House of Delegates of the American Massage Therapy Association, and a member of Associated Bodywork & Massage Professionals. I personally strive to be an advocate for education. I'm thankful my own education didn't stop at the massage school door; it began there. I not only love teaching, I love taking classes as well. I learn something new every day, and I appreciate the opportunity to share some of what I've learned.

Ryan Hoyme, aka TheMassageNerd

When I started teaching massage, I got interviewed on a Friday and started teaching on Monday. I didn't have any experience in teaching; the only experience I had was being a massage therapist for three years. I was scared to death my first day, and was even more intimidated that it was a class of 25 women. I wanted to quit every day that first quarter, but I hung in there because my dad was a 5th-grade teacher all his working career and I didn't want to disappoint him. I have been teaching full-time since January 2001, and I'm glad I stuck it out. Teaching has been the most rewarding career I could imagine.

In 2006, I started massagenerd.com and created my youtube channel, basically for my massage students. I never imagined that it would become the largest massage website on the Internet, averaging 150,000 views a day, accompanied by my youtube channel, with more massage videos than any other place on the World Wide Web. The website has over 25,000 pages, more than 3000 test questions, over 3000 videos, plus information on numerous other massage-related topics. I'm starting to branch out into other areas of holistic health like chiropractic, yoga and more, because I just love to share information.

I try to attend as many massage conferences as possible and at each one, interview as many educators as I can. I've appeared on numerous webinars, been a speaker at many conventions, and I host a weekly massage show on www.massagenerd.tv. I started that show in early 2010 and am usually booked at least 6 months in advance with different guests and topics. It's a great way to get educated and to virtually meet some of the great minds in the massage world. If you've searched for any massage information on the Internet, you've

probably viewed the website or massage videos. Massage students are
what make me strive to share as much as possible. The
students are our future and they're hungry for knowledge

Introduction

There are big differences in the way massage schools are operated. There are schools that have six students, and schools that have sixty in a single class. There are schools where everyone is wearing white scrubs, and schools where the students are allowed to wear cut-off jeans and attend in their bare feet. There are schools where the tuition is $3000 and schools where the tuition is $10,000 or more. There are schools that are located in inner-city warehouse lofts, and schools that are in beautiful pastoral settings.

No two schools are exactly alike—even within corporate chains and community college systems. The attitudes and goals, along with the finances and management style of the owner—or in the case of community colleges, the program director and administration, dictate which type of place it's going to be.

One thing that has been a constant: We can go into any school to teach a class, and by the end of the day, we'll have a feel for what level of organization is carried out in that particular school. It's evident in the attitudes and demeanor of the students, the instructors and administrators, and even the décor and layout of physical space. A well-organized school is easy to spot, and so is one that's poorly organized. In the latter, there is sometimes oblivion, and sometimes complacency at fault. Maybe they just don't know there's a better way, or they're stuck in the mode of maintaining the status quo.

When I (Laura Allen) was still new to the field of massage therapy, licensing came into my state (North Carolina). I saw school owners that I knew scrambling hard to comply with the new rules. Most of them were small operations started by good people who had great intentions. Community colleges hadn't really gotten on the massage bandwagon yet.

There was a huge lack of record keeping that carried over to the students who were educated in such places. There were repercussions as some schools closed and a whole generation of therapists, some of whom had been practicing for many years, had a hard time getting in under the grandfather clause, either due to poor record-keeping on the part of the school, or sometimes on the part of themselves, like a failure to keep client documentation such as intake forms or good progress notes. If you didn't have sufficient proof of having performed at least 400 documented massages over a four-year period, you couldn't take advantage of the grandfather clause.

Although the majority of states now have regulation of massage therapy, many of them still don't keep a very close watch on massage schools. Reading the practice acts in different states reveals a wide variance in how far boards go in policing education and making sure that students are getting the best entry-level start into the profession. A word to the wise: that can change at any time. When a massage board is still in their first decade of operation, they don't want to bite off more than they can chew. When the sunset period comes, that's a prime time for state legislatures to make changes in the law, and state boards are prohibited from lobbying for what they want or deem best. That is up to the professional associations, their government relations representatives, and whatever lobbyist they can afford to pay. Just because your school isn't regulated, or subject to regular review and inspection right now doesn't mean it won't be in the future.

Part I of *The Massage Education Manual* is directed at school owners and will also be helpful to key administrative personnel. Chapter 1 addresses the ethics of owning a massage school. Chapter 2 discusses the traditional Four P's of marketing: Product, Price, Place, and Promotion, and the business plan for your massage school. We're adding a fifth "P," *People*. In this Internet age, social and business relationships are much easier to maintain. Building relationships—not just herding students through a program—is paramount to having your graduates as walking advertisements for the excellence of your school. This is not a marketing book; however, you do have to market your school if you hope to attract and keep students. Chapter 2 also discusses curriculum choices for your school, as those have an impact on your business plan. Chapter 3 is about hiring and training competent instructors and staff members, and Chapter 4 is about creating your school's policies and procedures.

Part II of this book addresses record keeping and how to turn into a great record-keeper. Chapter 5 discusses the things you need to document as a member of the school administrative staff and faculty. Standardized forms for almost any need in the administration and business of running a massage school are referenced in this chapter and appear in Appendix I. They can be easily customized to include your letterhead and to fit your particular school or classroom. If you operate a school in a state that is regulated, be sure to check your particular state's requirements for school documentation. Your state board may go so far as to provide certain mandated forms.

The same holds for schools seeking accreditation from entities such as COMTA (Commission on Massage Therapy Accreditation). Depending on the accrediting body, there may be unique forms that you are required to use in place of or in addition to what is included in the book. If you operate in a state that does not yet have licensure, be aware that having proper documentation will serve you well if that day ever comes—and will still serve you well even if it never does. Your school will function much more efficiently if everyone on your staff is on the same page with their record-keeping practices.

Part III of this book is meant for the instructors. Teaching is a calling, but it's also a skill and a talent. You not only need to be a subject matter expert in the area you're teaching; you need to be an effective manager, and part entertainer. A sense of humor in the classroom goes a long way. You have to be able to impart knowledge in a way that's engaging enough to hold the students' interest. This section includes teaching strategies that will assist you in addressing all learning styles, as well as writing and organizing good syllabi and lesson plans. The special ethics considerations associated with teaching in a massage school are also discussed. Chapter 6 is a review of the basic elements of teaching. Chapter 7 is a discussion of classroom management. Chapter 8 is filled with tips for teaching, gleaned from our years of experience as teachers—and as students in the school of hard knocks. Chapter 9 discusses teaching online, including the necessary skills, benefits and challenges associated with distance learning. Chapter 10 contains information on how to become a provider of continuing education. Chapter 11 is a discussion of how to reach your full potential as an educator.

The appendices are a series of resources for school directors and teachers. Appendix I includes the previously mentioned sample forms. Appendix II includes contact information for state massage therapy boards. Appendix III includes contact information for national massage therapy organizations. Appendix IV contains research resources. Appendix V contains a listing of teacher training programs.

We don't want you to just run a massage school or just show up and teach every day. We want you to have a great time doing it! We want your job to be so much fun and so rewarding that you can't wait to get there every day.

This book is meant to help you do that by giving you guidelines for the tedious parts of the business, so your focus can be on the student. You're training students to help in healing the world, one body at a time. That should be a wonderful experience for all concerned—you and them, and ultimately, the clients they will serve.

In order for your school to prosper, you have to consistently turn out students who prosper as well. A high pass rate on state and national exams should be your goal; while the ability to pass a standardized test isn't a sign of talent as a massage therapist, it's currently what we have to rely on, and it's the sign that you are preparing your students to do what they must in order to be able to practice. We hope this manual will be helpful to you in organizing your school so that it operates in the most positive and creative way, so that you'll manifest prosperity by attracting all the students you want and be able to give them an optimal educational experience. Good Luck!

TABLE OF CONTENTS

Laura Allen and Ryan Hoyme

Part I

Your Own Massage School

There are two kinds of people, those who do the work and those who take the credit for it. Try to be in the first group; there's less competition there.
~Indira Gandhi

Chapter 1

The Ethics of Massage School Ownership

The nature of what we do as massage therapists—placing our hands on unclothed people—dictates that we must follow a code of professional ethics. Most states that have licensing for massage therapists have a code of ethics; the national bodywork and massage associations have codes of their own. Some school owners choose to write, or adapt, a code of their own.

The buck stops here—ultimately, as the school owner, it is your business plan and your wishes that must be followed, your policies and procedures that must be adhered to, your staff that has to be trained, and your students that must be attended to. You have a moral obligation to conduct your business in an ethical manner, but more so, to *model* ethical behavior that will filter down through your administrative staff and instructors to your students. To borrow a phrase from Dr. Ben Benjamin, the sports medicine expert, author and massage therapist, *you are not apt to behave any more ethically in your business than you do in your private life.*

So true; and yet, life is full of paradoxes. What is illegal may not necessarily be immoral, and what is immoral is relative to whom you're talking. In order for you to be sure you are modeling professional and ethical behavior for your staff and students, you may need to take a fearless and searching moral inventory of yourself, for it is *your* character and *your* sense of ethics that is going to be on display and setting the tone for all who enter your school.

Models of Business Ethics

In the business world, there have traditionally been two main models of ethics, the stakeholder model and the shareholder model. In the stakeholder model, the needs and desires of four main groups of people are considered: the investors, employees, suppliers, and customers. In the shareholder model of business, the shareholder(s) being the owner(s) of the business, the firm put their interests first, with emphasis on increasing value and profit for them. David Rodin of the Center for Applied Philosophy and Public Ethics of Australian National University has proposed a third model, the *ownership* model of business ethics. The ownership model places more emphasis on the rights and responsibilities of the owner than previous models. Rodin acknowledges that in many businesses, the owner and the manager may be two different people, and stresses that there may be moral obligations incumbent upon the owner that do not necessarily apply to the manager. Operating your school in an ethical manner is insurance that you are complying with all laws, avoiding any circumstances that could result in a civil or criminal action being brought against you and/or any of your personnel, and maintaining an image of integrity in the eyes of the public.

Your Ethical Responsibilities to Your Students

Ethically speaking, you have a number of responsibilities to your students. If you are holding your establishment out as a place of learning that will prepare them for a career in the massage therapy profession, you should be adhering to the laws of your state, if there are any, governing such schools. Students should have the expectation that they are attending a school that at a minimum is in compliance with any accreditation or legal requirements. If you are operating in a state that has no guidelines specifically for massage schools, borrow from what is expected of those training others in the medical profession, such as a school of nursing or physical therapy, or look to other massage schools to see what they are doing.

You have a responsibility to advertise your school in an ethical manner. That means no promises of jobs that will supposedly automatically appear once your students graduate; no claims of "free" massage tables or other such equipment, when in fact it is not free but factored in to the cost of the program; no misleading claims about your school's pass rate on the licensing exams that may be required; no wild proclamations that graduates from your school get hired more often than the graduates of the school across town because everyone knows your place is superior. If your school is in reality superior, the word will get out, and you will not have to make such claims. Better that they should hear it from someone else instead of the person with the most vested interest.

Anything that is stated or implied in your catalog, your student handbook, on your website, or in any other advertising, should be the absolute truth and not be misleading in any way. We once visited a school in that we had received a color catalog from in the mail. On the cover of the catalog was a picture of the school, at the foot of a gorgeous green and majestic mountain with a distinctive peak. Imagine our surprise, on the way to that school when we passed that mountain about fifteen miles before getting to the school. They had superimposed the picture of the school onto the picture of the mountain (and in fact named the school after the mountain). True, it was within reasonably close proximity, but we were still incredulous at the misrepresentation, and we bet more than one student was surprised on their first visit to find that the school was in fact located on the busy highway, and not in the lovely mountain meadow they were led to believe.

Financial Ethics

You have financial responsibility for your school. Laws vary from state to state, but some accrediting agencies and some states require educational institutions to be bonded. Regulatory boards and accrediting entities also usually require regular audits or financial reviews by an impartial and qualified person, such as a CPA (Certified Public Accountant). Whether required by law or not, you have an ethical responsibility to keep enough cash on hand so that every student that is enrolled is assured of graduation—in other words, enough money in the bank to meet all expenses, including rent, utilities, laundry, advertising, supplies, textbooks, and any other expense associated with keeping the wheels of progress turning for the students who are already there.

Students should have the expectation that they are going to receive the education they paid for, regardless of whether that payment came out of their pocket or in the form of a government grant or student loan. And unless you're Donald Trump, you can't afford to ignore your business affairs in any case. If someone other than yourself keeps the books, it's very unwise on your part not to keep abreast of the financial health of your school. We've had the experience of seeing schools go bankrupt—in one case when the students were only two weeks away from graduation. The students showed up for class to find that the landlord had padlocked the building—with their massage tables and other personal belongings inside—because of the owner falling months behind on the rent. It was a nightmare for the students. The state's massage board intervened and conducted a teach-out for the students, but no student should have to suffer through such an event.

Ethical and Qualified Educators

You have a responsibility to staff your enterprise with ethical and qualified people. Paying a manager to run your school, if you don't have the time, skills, or inclination is your choice, but if there were a lawsuit for any reason against any of your personnel it would undoubtedly come back to you, as the owner of the business. You have a responsibility to employ administration that is competent, and teachers that are qualified.

In some states, one must submit to a criminal record check in order to get a massage license; some feel this is picking on massage therapists, but the rule often applies to other health care practitioners as well, who have the opportunity to treat people who are in a vulnerable position. You may be the world's most trusting person, but it is smart business sense to require the same of any staff you employ. When hiring instructional staff who should be licensed massage therapists, check your state board's website for verification of their license and any disciplinary actions. Require adequate documentation of the qualifications they claim to have. Don't take their word for it. That may sound harsh, but it's necessary.

Never forget that we are in the business of placing our hands on unclothed people. You cannot err too far on the side of caution with your choice of staff. You would not want an administrator who turned out to be a wife-beater, and you would feel pretty ignorant if you didn't know that until it was in the paper that he'd been arrested for the fourth time for domestic abuse. You do not want someone who has been arrested for stealing or served time for fraud or embezzlement handling the money in your business.

People can and do make positive changes in their lives, and the person who committed a crime twenty years ago and has been leading an exemplary life ever since may be a great person for your administrative job opening, but you might be concerned about someone who just committed a crime in the past year or two. Check the references of everyone you hire. By law, former employers are not allowed to tell you very much about your candidate—but they can tell you whether or not the person is eligible to be rehired, and you should always ask that question when you call for a reference.

Ethical and Fair Treatment of Students

You have an ethical responsibility to treat all students with respect, and to see to it that your staff does the same—and the responsibility for seeing that the students respect each other. Zero tolerance for sexual harassment, and for discrimination based on gender, race, sexual preference, ethnicity, religion, or any other reason is the only acceptable path to follow.

You also have a responsibility to make sure your school complies with the Americans with Disabilities Act, which guarantees equal access to education for those with handicaps and requires that you make reasonable accommodations to assist physically, mentally or emotionally challenged students. Your school must be fully accessible to handicapped people, with a wheelchair ramp, or elevator if located other than on the first floor. A student must be allowed to bring in their service animal, if they have one.

Quality, Not Quantity

You have a responsibility to provide students with the physical facility and equipment necessary to train them for a career in massage therapy. Many states spell this out in their practice act or rules by stating that there must be *x* number of square feet per student, exclusive of fixed furnishings. Ten square feet is an average requirement. This is an important rule. A massage table is six feet long and around thirty or so inches wide, and the student must have room to move around. Students shouldn't be bumping into each other during clinical practice; you can hardly teach proper body mechanics if they don't have the room to practice them in, and it's not conducive to a good educational experience. Some school owners are only interested in the bottom line—*if I get x number of students, I can make a million a year*—without regard for the needs and comforts of students and staff. You will reap more financial and personal rewards by leaving some growing room.

In addition to adequate room to move around, there should be equipment that is kept clean and in good repair. Bear in mind that a massage table is just like a car, it needs a tune-up every now and then. The screws and cables may need tightening. Floors should be clean and free from obstruction. All instructional and public areas should be spotless. If you can't afford a cleaning service, and you're not into scrubbing, offer work-study to a student to clean the building in exchange for reduced tuition. Adequate lighting is a must. An adequate number of tables and chairs should be on hand. There seems to be a trend in some massage schools we have visited to have the students sit on the floor. We're not sure of the motivation behind that, whether it's to save money or space by not purchasing tables and chairs, but not everyone is comfortable sitting on the floor, especially for hours at a time. Revisit that plan.

Part of equipping your school should include a student reference library. It should contain every textbook used or referenced in your curriculum and as much more as your finances allow you to provide.

Ethical Policies and Procedures

Finally, you have the responsibility to create and implement policies and procedures for your school, and ultimately, to see that they're adhered to by everyone *including you*. Bear in mind that when students enter your school, they are subject to the published policies as they existed at the time they entered. For instance, if your catalog stated that students need six hundred actual hours of class attendance in order to graduate, you can't suddenly change that to seven hundred after they have already started their education. You may change policies to be effective to new students coming in, but the ones who are already there should have the expectation of finishing under the same circumstances they started under. If you're already a school owner, you hopefully have policies and procedures in place. If you're just thinking of opening a school, you're going to be surprised at what a long document your policies and procedures manual will turn out to be. There's a lot to address. Policies and Procedures are covered thoroughly in Chapter 4.

Chapter 2

Massage Education: It's a Business

Massage therapists are often an idealistic bunch. They're frequently in the "I'm just here to help people" mode, even when making a living is a necessity, like it is for most of us. Although there are exceptions to the rule, most people who start a massage school are therapists themselves. A successful school is one that is turning out students who are well educated and well prepared for the massage therapy profession—*and making money for the owner*. And while there's no doubt that most school owners start out with the desire to help others learn the best job in the world—helping people feel better—don't lose sight of the fact that it's a business. Treat it like one.

The Five P's: Product, Price, Place, Promotion, and People

The Four P's (a term traditionally used in marketing textbooks) are intrinsically linked together. We've expanded on that by adding a fifth "P," *People*—the reason for everything we do. We educate *people*. The consumers of massage are *people*. Whatever you are considering doing in your business—your massage school—you have to consider how it is going to affect the *people* involved in your decision.

In this business venture, *education is the product*. That's not a singular entity; it's the combination of attributes and characteristics that will make your school a unique and desirable place for students to spend their time and money. The quality of education your students receive will have a direct impact on their marketability to employers and their chances of success in the profession.

Think realistically for a moment about the characteristics of your massage school. Why is your school any better than the next? Is it more affordable to the masses, or more convenient, location- or schedule-wise? Do you have well-known instructors who are published (which is definitely not a necessity, but is a good selling point)? Is the curriculum different from what your competitors are offering (over and above what's required by the state)? Are you offering financial aid, job placement services, and internship opportunities? All those factors add up to your product—*your brand*.

Place refers to not only your physical location, which is certainly important, but also to your position in the marketplace. If your school is the only one for miles around, you're in a great position. If it's not, how do you plan to claim your share of the career education market? It's a selling point if you're in a location that's convenient to public transportation...but the opposite is true as well. Some successful schools are in such remote locations they have lodging available for students, and those appeal to a different target market.

If you're thinking of opening a school in a small town or rural area, be realistic about whether or not that's going to be sustainable. You could attract students from out of your area—if you spend the money to advertise out of your area. If your only advertising is in the local paper, that's not going to attract those students who live out of your immediate proximity, and just a few graduating classes could saturate your area with massage therapists competing for a limited audience. You want your school to have longevity, and location and the demographics there need to be considered.

Price, to some students, is the deciding factor in whether or not to attend a certain school, if there's more than one local choice. That doesn't mean you should strive to offer the lowest tuition in town. People often have the perception "you get what you pay for," and most of the time, that's true. Pricing yourself at half what the competing school across town charges could backfire and give the impression that you're not offering an education of comparable (or better) value.

Community colleges tend to have lower tuition costs than private schools, and they also all have financial aid opportunities available to students. Many proprietary schools can't compete with that. The student who is looking for a more unique education is going to look for a private school. Not to detract from the community college experience in any way, but those programs often include requirements that you won't see in a private school, such as regular college classes in math, English, and other classes that the student might not be looking forward to—and in some instances, there's a semester or two of such classes before massage education begins in earnest, or the student even gets to touch a body. Private schools usually skip those general education classes and get right into the nuts and bolts of massage therapy education.

Community colleges are also subsidized by taxpayer money, and private schools can't make that claim. The price you settle on for tuition should be enough to make your school financially viable. It's noble to want your tuition to be low enough to be affordable to everyone, but on the other hand, you have to meet your overhead and presumably make a living as well. Remember that as you are working out your budget—and also remember to have a contingency plan in the event you don't attract as many students as you were hoping to.

Promoting your school is going to encompass all the previous points. You want to cast your school in the best light possible, by highlighting the strengths of your business plan and using those as your marketing points. You want to get the biggest return on investment for your advertising dollars. Ultimately, you want word of mouth to be your best advertising, but you can't depend on that in the first year or two of operation, until you have some satisfied graduates who can recommend your school—and they have satisfied clients to recommend them.

Advertising is an expense that is easy to snowball out of control. You can't afford to go broke attempting to get students—but you do need to get them—so be realistic when you are creating your budget. It's tempting to advertise in every venue that's available, but it's not smart. It's a necessity to shop around for advertising venues that will reach the most potential students for the least amount of money. Hosting career days at your school isn't going to cost you much, and should be a regular part of your marketing efforts. The same for career days held at local high schools. Participate!

Many massage schools have stopped printing catalogs altogether and instead direct all inquiries to their websites. Having a professionally-designed, search-engine optimized, regularly updated website is a necessity. There are also numerous information websites out there for massage therapists and potential attendees, and your school should appear on as many of them as possible. It's the nature of the Internet that the more hits a website gets, the closer to the top of the search engine list it's going to be. It's also the nature of compilation-type websites, and sites like the Yellow Pages to list schools in alphabetical order, so having a school name that starts with an "A" may serve you to start with, but after a period of time, the school with the website that gets more hits will come out at the top of search engines.

And so, it all comes back to *people*: your educational offerings; the price, the place, and the promotion. Define your target market—the people you want to reach, and that is the starting point for what you're going to offer them, how you're going to reach them, and the kind of relationships you're going to build with them. Satisfied students become satisfied graduates. With the popularity of social media, including review websites, word will get around quickly if your students feel they're getting the education they deserve—or not.

Keep these Five P's in mind as you work on creating (or revising) your business plan.

The Business Plan

The first thing you need to develop for your massage school, if you haven't already, is a business plan. If you're already open for business and everything has been going fine and profitably for you for the past five years or longer, then good for you. If that's not the case, it's never too late to write a plan—or to revisit your old one. Things change—like the economy, or the demographics of your students. Say you start out in one location and a few years later, move to another one. Even a move across town can change the number and type of students you'll attract. It's a good idea to review your business plan annually to see what's still working, and what isn't.

People sometimes think if they're not going to the bank to borrow money, that they don't need a plan. That's a mistake. And if you are going to the bank to borrow money, showing up without a written plan is the quickest way to ensure that you'll be turned down for the loan. Having a written plan gives you a set of guidelines to follow on the way to meeting your goals. It's a written summary of your purposes for going into business, what you hope to accomplish, and the strategies you'll use to help you realize those goals.

There are a number of components to a business plan:
- ➤ The executive summary
- ➤ A list of the objectives for your school
- ➤ The mission statement
- ➤ The keys to success—a list of strengths that will potentially make your venture a successful one
- ➤ Highlights of the company—what will make it stand out from other schools in your area
- ➤ Biographical information about the owner(s)
- ➤ The budget—your projected income and expenses for at least one year, preferably five years
- ➤ Information about different types of programs and/or other services you might offer, such as massage in a student clinic and continuing education classes
- ➤ A market study and market survey analysis
- ➤ Marketing strategies that you intend to use to attract students

The **executive summary** is going to be the first part of the plan—and the last thing you'll write. The executive summary is used to highlight the key points of your plan, and will be used as the introduction once you finish the other parts of it.

A **list of objectives** for your school would include what it is you want to accomplish and provide for your students. In states that regulate schools, this will definitely need to be in compliance with those regulations; for example, regarding the number of hours of required education.

The list might look similar to this:

- ☐ To provide a 650-hour comprehensive education in massage therapy.
- ☐ To hire instructors who have at least five years of experience for hands-on classes.
- ☐ To hire instructors who have a minimum of an undergraduate degree in science-based classes.
- ☐ To prepare students for working in the field of massage therapy in a variety of different settings, by partnering with local businesses to provide internship opportunities

Your list may be much longer. Bear in mind, your plan is going to be just as unique as your school. You may be planning a small, intimate class size of 6 students, or planning on a much larger enrollment. Your business plan needs to reflect your hopes and dreams—along with a healthy dose of reality. Planning on being profitable in the first year or two is usually a gross miscalculation—and could even make the bank say thanks, but no thanks, if you're seeking a loan. Loan officers would prefer to see a realistic projection of the facts than a dressed-up version of how wildly successful you'll be as soon as you open the doors. They would probably be much more willing to lend money to someone who projects a loss in the first two years than they would someone who is claiming they'll make a $50,000 profit in the first year.

The next component of the plan is the mission statement. Here is the mission statement borrowed from the Asheville School of Massage & Yoga:

The Asheville School of Massage & Yoga believes that a supportive and nurturing environment within the framework of a rigorous course of study is crucial to personal, professional, and academic success. It is the school's mission to provide a caring place in which students, faculty, staff, and Asheville's community members can learn and grow in this very special field of study.

My (Laura Allen) own mission statement says:

We are body workers and educators who seek to serve our community and beyond by honoring the human body and spirit of everyone who comes through our door, in the belief that the awesome power of touch can change the world, one person at a time.

That's all there is to it; write a sentence or two with your unique outlook.

Keys to success are the strengths that will make your school successful. For example, if the owner has a proven track record in education, business management, and finance, or has assembled a team that does, that's a good strength. It could be that the building is owned free and clear—and thus less worries about making ends meet. It could be that you've already announced—and filled—your first class.

Highlights of the company are the things that will make your school stand out from other institutions. It may be that the school is the only one within a certain geographic area, or the only one offering financial aid to students. It may be that there is something unique about the school. The Asheville School of Massage & Yoga mentioned above is a good example; yoga is incorporated into every class, and upon graduation, the student is qualified as both a massage therapist and a yoga instructor. That's a selling point. Having an evening or weekend program will appeal to working people.

Biographical information about the owner should focus on the qualifications that will inspire confidence: education, experience, and expertise in the field.

The budget is one of the most important parts of the business plan. Unless you possess unlimited funds, you should err on the side of caution by being conservative in your projections of income, and realistic when projecting expenses—and then some. Time and space will dictate how many students you can accommodate in your program at one time. You may have the space for 20—but what if you only attract 15? You should be financially stable enough to weather periods of low enrollment and unexpected expenses. People don't usually plan for recession—but they should. A recession has occurred in regular cycles for more 200 years. According to Wikipedia, 11 recessions occurred between 1949 and 2001 alone. Be certain that economics don't put you out of business before you get off to a good start.

Your budget will need to be revisited, and probably revised, on an ongoing basis when you first start your business. Checking bills and income monthly will keep you on top of where you've been and where you're going financially. Bear in mind that there will be startup expenses, possible security deposits, and equipment purchases when you first start out that can be amortized and depreciated. It's wise to pay an accountant or tax professional to handle that, even if you've had prior experience figuring your own personal tax. A call to the utility companies can get you the information of how much the cost has historically been in your building, if you are starting in an existing structure. Preparing a five-year projection will demonstrate commitment that you intend on having longevity.

Information about your offerings. Your plan should include all the sources of income you plan to have in addition to tuition. If you plan to offer continuing education classes, have a student book and supply store, sell massage tables, have a student clinic and/or professional clinic, include those details.

Market survey and analysis should take into account how many other massage schools/programs are available within easy driving distance—and how many career opportunities there are for therapists in your area. Take into account the number of chiropractic offices, day spas, and resorts in the area that could potentially employ massage therapists. You can only estimate how many people would go into business for themselves; according to ABMP's research, that's more than 75%. If your location is in a small town and your students are from your local area, which is likely to be the case unless there is something unique about your school that would entice students to drive some distance to attend, then it might not take you long to saturate the market. You want your school to last longer than a year or two, so be diligent with your market survey when planning your class sizes and length of your program. Six new graduates hitting the job market every year in a small town may be sustainable, but if you're graduating a class of 20 every six months, that may not.

Marketing strategies are the methods you'll use to attract new students. These will include your website, print ads, radio and television, direct mailing, career days and open houses at your facility. Advertising is one of those expenses that is easy to let get out of hand. Be particularly careful with this area of your budget, and track your return on investment. Use a tracking sheet with all your marketing efforts listed on it, and each time potential students contact you, ask them how they heard about the school. Bear in mind that one advertisement isn't apt to attract much attention; advertising needs to be consistent. However, if you've tried a certain advertising venue for 60-90 days and haven't had any results from that, it's time to switch gears and spend your advertising dollars somewhere else.

Below is a sample business plan.

Business Plan for the Body of Knowledge School of Massage

> **The executive summary (remember, although this is at the beginning, it is written last and then inserted at the beginning.)**

The Body of Knowledge School of Massage has a sound business plan. The owner is bringing a wealth of experience and has sufficient financial resources. The market in this area is sufficient to support the advanced type of training the school will offer. The availability of classes on nights and weekends in addition to traditional daytime classes will attract students who work, since it will make it much easier for them to work out a schedule that will suit their individual needs. The availability of private financing will enable students without sufficient existing financial resources to attend. The recently renovated building is equipped with state of the art technology. A well-rounded marketing program will attract students from this county and surrounding areas.

Keep in mind, the summary doesn't need to repeat the whole plan; just hit the high points.

> **A list of the objectives for your school**

The objectives for the Body of Knowledge School of Massage are to:
- Provide a 1000-hour educational program in massage therapy.
- Attract highly qualified instructors who are experts in their subject matter areas.
- Achieve an enrollment of 20 students twice per six-month cycle.

- Offer night and weekend classes to accommodate working adults.
- Meet the standards expected by COMTA for accreditation during the first three years of operation.

Your school will have it's own unique objectives, and you should spell those out.

➢ The mission statement

Our mission is to provide superior education, so that we may provide the public with superior massage therapists. We honor the individuality of each student who enters our door.

➢ The keys to success—a list of strengths that will potentially make your venture a successful one

- The owner has many years of previous experience in the management of a chain of corporate career colleges.
- The building is located in a formerly depressed area that is undergoing urban revitalization with very promising growth, and was purchased at a bargain price.
- The owner has arranged with a private loan company to offer financing to qualified students.
- The owner has sufficient liquid operating capital to sustain the school for a period of three years, and investors who are willing to contribute additional funding if needed.

➢ Highlights of the company—what will make it stand out from other schools in your area

- The availability of day, night, and weekend classes will make the program accessible to everyone.
- The other school in the immediate area only offers a 500-hour program, which is the minimum the state requires. Our longer program will appeal to the student who desires a more thorough education that will give them a competitive advantage in the job market.
- The facility has been newly renovated and furnished with state of the art technology and equipment.
- Four medical facilities have agreed to provide internship opportunities for students.

➢ **Biographical information about the owner(s)**
Bob Beckensale has over 20 years of experience as the executive director of a chain of career colleges. He has been involved in all aspects of the company, including hiring staff and faculty, overseeing curriculum development, expanding the scope of career offerings, and the other aspects of managing a successful multi-location education franchise. He has an MBA from Duke University and is a graduate of the Rolf Institute.

➢ **The budget—your projected income and expenses for at least one year, preferably five years**

A sample budget form appears in Table 2-1.

Remember that depending on how you choose to run things in your particular school, there may be additional expenses. For example, you may pay wholesale prices for textbooks, massage tables and so forth and resell them at retail to your students, or you may require them to buy them on their own.

Another thing to keep in mind, if you're planning on borrowing money to finance your venture, is that loan officers don't want to see any grandiose projections of profit during the first couple of years of operation. It isn't going to happen! The bank would much rather see a realistic projection of loss—and in fact— usually expect any business venture to operate in the red for the first couple of years.

That doesn't mean they won't take a chance on lending you money, and in fact, they're more likely to if they can see that you are not suffering from the "instant profit" syndrome. Few businesses of any kind can open and start making an instant profit, and that kind of unreasonable expectation is the main reason many new ventures don't even last a year.

Table 2-1. Sample budget form.

Expense	Projected Monthly Amount	Actual Monthly Amount	- or +	Total for Year_____
Rent or mortgage				
Electricity				
Gas				
Water				
Telephone				
Internet access				
Property insurance				
Liability insurance				
Office supplies				
Janitorial supplies				
Cleaning service				
Professional memberships				
Advertising				
Repairs and maintenance				
Retail sales tax				
Property tax				
Salaries and wages				
Taxes payable on salaries and wages				
Massage equipment				
Massage Products for in-house use				
Office equipment				
Laundry				
Miscellaneous				
Total				

Your budget will also need to reflect projected income.

Projected Income	Projected Monthly Amount	Actual Monthly Amount	- or +	Total for Year_____
Tuition				
Student Clinic				
Book sales				
Massage table sales				
CE Classes				
Total				

One of the most important steps in creating your budget is to have a contingency plan. If you have planned for *x* number of students, and you don't attract that number, will you still be able to open the school or keep it running?

> **Information about different types of programs and/or other services you might offer, such as massage in a student clinic and continuing education classes**

   ☐ Massage will be available in the student clinic 6 days per week.
   ☐ Continuing education classes will be offered approximately once per month.

> **A market study and market survey analysis**

   A review of the market has shown that there is only one other massage school within a 50-mile radius. It offers a 500-hour program; our school will offer a 1000-hour program.

> **Marketing strategies that you intend to use to attract students**

The school will be advertised through a number of different avenues, including a professionally-designed and administrated website that offers a downloadable catalog and online registration; advertisements will also appear in the Sunday editions of newspapers within a 50-mile radius; print ads will also appear in the monthly editions of Holistic Health Magazine, a regional publication distributed in six counties; a commercial will appear on the local cable information channel, and two billboard advertisements have been purchased on both major highways that enter the town. Additionally, we plan to be a presence at local and surrounding area high school career days, festivals, and health fairs.

This is one example of a business plan. Use it as a guide for creating your own plan, and once it's complete, highlight the components into one shorter statement—the executive summary, and place it at the beginning of your plan.

Beyond the Business Plan: Curriculum

The curriculum you choose to offer in your school certainly affects your business plan in several ways. The first consideration is of course being in compliance with your state board and/or accrediting agency, if they mandate the teaching of certain subjects and/or require a minimum number of hours in specific areas of instruction. Curriculum may also affect how many instructors you need to hire, and how much education they may be required to have in order to teach the subject. That should be taken into account when you are negotiating and budgeting for teacher salaries; someone with a master's degree or doctorate, or another licensed professional such as a chiropractor or physical therapist will generally require more salary than a person with a high school diploma and a massage diploma.

Curriculum requirements vary from state to state, if the governing board has bothered to spell that out, and many have. That variance is responsible for many of the problems in licensing portability. For comparison's sake, Table 2-2 illustrates the difference in the educational requirements of two states, New York and North Carolina.

Table 2-2. Required hours of study.

Subject Area	New York Required Clock Hours of Study	North Carolina Required Clock Hours of Study
Anatomy & Physiology	200, including 50 hours of neurology	100
Myology and/or Kinesiology	150	
Pathology	100	Included in A&P requirement
Hygiene, First Aid, and other areas related to the practice of massage	75	
Theory and techniques of massage	150, including the study of Oriental massage and at least 50 hours of instruction in each type of massage therapy taught	200, at least 100 of which must be hands-on
Additional massage therapy techniques	325, including at least 150 hours of hands-on practical onsite supervision	150, no more than 100 of which may be supervised practice; no more than 50 hours may be in techniques exempt from licensure (e.g., energy work)
Ethics		15
Business Management		15
Psychological concepts related to massage		20
Total hours	1000	500

If you're still in the planning phase prior to opening your massage school, we encourage you to plan your curriculum carefully. At a minimum, a well-rounded massage education is going to include anatomy and physiology, pathology and contraindications, kinesiology, body mechanics, professional ethics, business practices, and massage theory and practice. The teaching of research literacy isn't required in any state we're aware of—but it should be. If you want to prepare students to work with physicians and other health care providers, you must teach the evidence-informed practice of massage, and more hard-core science. Many states give a lot of leeway with curriculum, with some stating in their rules something along the lines of "100 hours of adjunct modalities may be taught", and some schools offering elective courses for those or just putting whatever personally appeals to the owner in the mix.

The study of professional ethics and the jurisprudence of your own state laws should be given ample hours...the 15 hours required in my state (Laura Allen) barely touched the tip of the iceberg. You can't expect to turn out massage therapists who will be ethical and law-abiding practitioners if they are not well-educated in these areas.

As mentioned in the business plan, your curriculum may be what makes your school stand out from others. While some take the intensive study approach to one or two modalities, other schools operate like a smorgasboard, giving students just enough training in a modality to introduce them to it...or to be incompetent at it. We've had the experience of seeing a teacher do an 8-hour class in reflexology and then telling the students they should list reflexology on their advertising—not a good idea.

Remember that *your* business plan is not the only one to consider. Teaching students how to write an effective business plan is a must. The statistics from the professional associations (which always disagree with each other to some extent) show that about 60,000 people a year enter the profession, and about that same number go out. True, some of them leave to retire, or some have career-ending injuries, but just as many leave because they are not adequately prepared for the business of massage. Be sure that your curriculum prepares students for the real world—skip the promises that they're going to get out of school and immediately start making $75 an hour. It isn't going to happen. They need to understand a business plan as well as you do. They need to be taught budgeting, taxes and other legal responsibilities, and how to effectively market themselves.

The One-Man (or Woman) Show

There are small massage schools across the country where one person is teaching the entire curriculum. We've been in some of them. One such owner informed us he was a subject matter expert in 28 different areas. That's hard to believe—but even if it's so, what would happen to the students in such a place if the sole instructor was run over by a bus or experienced a catastrophic illness?

If your business plan, and ergo your school, is based entirely upon your own talents, you need to have a backup plan securely in place as part of your business plan. It isn't fair to students who have invested their time and money to attend, only to have some unforeseen circumstance interfere with their education. Where will you find a substitute teacher who is also a subject matter expert in 28 areas? You're not likely to, so you'll need a bank of substitutes you can draw from in the event of an emergency. That needs to be in place before such an emergency happens.

The fact that one teacher is doing everything should also honestly be stated in your catalog and your advertising. One student from such a school stated that he would not have chosen the school he did if he had known everything was going to be taught by one person; that fact was misrepresented on the school's website, which listed several other instructors (that the owner said after the fact were no longer with the school and he just hadn't got around to changing the website) and the student stated to us that although he felt the owner was a competent teacher, he felt he would have gotten more out of the education by hearing more than one person's perspective.

Chapter 3

Hiring the Right People to Teach Your Students

As a school owner, one of your most important tasks will be to hire qualified teachers. If your state regulates massage schools, your licensing body probably goes so far as to spell out what that entails. If that isn't the case, bear in mind that your mission is to provide quality education. A textbook is just a book. A great teacher will make it come alive.

It's an unfortunate fact that many schools are guilty of hiring last year's graduates to be this year's teachers without so much as a day of training in how to be a good instructor. The problem with that is that no matter how talented at technique they may be, they are lacking in practical experience. It takes a few years of practice for a new graduate to become seasoned in working with all kinds of people, all kinds of bodies, and all kinds of conditions. It takes experience in dealing with ethical dilemmas, which anyone right out of school isn't going to have. If you have a graduate that you feel would make a promising instructor, don't just turn them loose on the class the month after they've gotten their license. Utilize them as a teaching assistant while they gain some on-the-job training.

It's important for any teacher to be a subject matter expert in the area in which he's going to teach, either through education, practical experience, or a combination of both. Can someone teach anatomy and physiology by just following a lesson plan in a teacher's textbook? Sure, but how effective will they be when a student asks a hard question and when open discussion is taking place in class? If a student asks the anatomy teacher where the pyloric sphincter is located, the teacher shouldn't have to look that up. A business and marketing teacher might have a degree in that area, which is good, but even better is someone with a degree who has actually run a business, and not someone who is just teaching right out of the book. There's just no substitute for practical experience.

Instructors who also have excellent knowledge of anatomy and physiology should teach the hands-on technique classes. Knowing the massage strokes is not enough. You can't say "Palpate the psoas" if you don't know where the psoas is.

It isn't enough to be a subject matter expert in the field. A good teacher is engaging as well as informative—part instructor, part entertainer. A good teacher recognizes that people have different learning preferences, and accommodates that. In the massage school environment, the instructor is teaching other adults—a different thing entirely from teaching school children. Massage schools are likely to attract a cross-section of students, including age-wise. An effective teacher is one who can relate good learning skills and good study skills to the students, as well as the subject at hand.

A teacher who just stands in front of the class lecturing all day is not going to hold students' interest. A well-rounded combination of lecture, demonstration, written exercises (or computer-based exercises, since many schools have gone paperless these days), PowerPoint presentations, supplemental videos, interactive discussion, and hands-on learning exercises will keep things interesting.

How do you know if an instructor is up to par before you hire one? Education and prior experience are certainly factors, but not the only things to consider. Checking references is important—to a point. Due to privacy laws, employers won't divulge much information. The all-important question is "Would your company consider this person eligible to be rehired?" You could ask if the teacher has any former students who would be willing to give a reference.

Google the instructor's name; you may find a message board with reviews on it. One bad review among a bunch of positives shouldn't be given any weight, but if there are more than a couple of bad reviews, particularly all complaining about the same thing, you'd want to pay attention to that. If five people say a teacher is boring or incompetent, then she probably is.

If your school is already in operation, you could ask the teacher to be a guest instructor as an audition. If the applicant has a previous record of teaching, chances are he may have a video of a class he's taught. If the person happens to be an approved provider of continuing education, as many instructors are, you could ask to see class evaluations and/or lesson plans from past classes.

Once you've hired an instructor, regular evaluations should be conducted, both by you and the students. Student evaluations should be conducted anonymously, so that there is no hesitance to be honest on the student's part and no fear of repercussions. There's bound to be one complainer in every crowd, but if more than one or two people have the same complaint about an instructor, chances are it's a viable complaint. It could be something as simple as talking too fast, or something as serious as sexual harassment—or heaven forbid, just not being perceived as knowledgeable about the subject at hand. A student told me (Laura Allen) once "my ethics teacher doesn't really like to talk about ethics, so we spend most of the time just talking about something else." That's a serious matter. At one point during my own education, I had an anatomy teacher who couldn't pronounce the terminology. He knew the names and locations of the muscles and was quite knowledgeable about it, but he butchered the language. That was a serious matter and he was eventually fired after a number of complaints.

You should have a written contract with your instructors and any administrative staff that is very specific about your expectations as far as performance of duties, causes for termination, any job benefits that are being offered, amount of notice expected should the instructor decide to leave, and even down to the dress code. By stating a probationary period of employment on the contract, you are covering yourself in the event the teacher turns out not to be a good fit for your school. A period of 1-3 months should be sufficient for you to determine if that's the case. If your school is on a modular, quarter, or semester system, you may want to set up the contract for one of those periods.

Look for teachers who are technology savvy—you don't want to hire someone who refuses to learn how to use PowerPoints, or who doesn't include new developments in the field in their class who offers the excuse "I'm just not computer-literate." Look for teachers who keep abreast of current research and who think it's important for students to be research literate. Question them about their own plans for personal development. Do they look forward to taking continuing education classes, or are they the "I already know it all" variety? Look for the former; avoid the latter at all costs.

Some state boards specify that providing regular teacher training for faculty is the obligation of the school owner. As the owner, you may not necessarily be an instructor yourself, and may be lacking in that particular area of expertise. If that's the case, hire someone to conduct your teacher training—and you'd be doing yourself a huge favor by educating yourself in that area, even if you don't intend to teach. Understanding adult learners, and at a minimum knowing what skills are needed to be an effective teacher—even if you don't possess them yourself—are vital to the success of your business. You can hardly hire excellent people to teach in your school if you don't know what constitutes that excellence.

Meet with your faculty frequently. Listen when they have concerns. Provide them with the tools they need to do their job. You can be a boss who's firm about expectations—but always willing to listen and consider other ideas. Be appreciative for the work people do for you. Be a good leader, model professionalism, and your staff will follow suit.

Chapter 4

Policies and Procedures

Policies and procedures serve several purposes. They provide a framework for the daily operation and activities of your business. They serve to let staff members and students know what is expected of them. Good policies and procedures can protect you in case of a lawsuit—reason enough in itself to write them down.

In order for policies and procedures to be effective, your employees and your students must be informed about them. Any policies and procedures affecting staff members and faculty should be listed in their employment contracts, or at a minimum, referenced in the contract and pointed toward the policy manual. Each employee and faculty member should be provided with a copy of the manual, and there should always be an easily accessible copy available in the school office.

Any policies and procedures affecting students should be clearly stated in the school's catalog and referenced in the enrollment agreement. Policies and procedures specific to any class should be stated on that particular syllabus.

The need for policies and procedures affecting staff could include, but may not be limited to:

- Absences from work
- Academic misconduct
- Attendance at staff meetings
- Benefits
- Causes for termination
- Confidentiality of business information
- Confidentiality of student information
- Continuing education/staff training requirements
- Disciplinary actions
- Dress code
- Ethics violations
- Grievance procedures
- Hiring
- Inclement weather plans
- Injuries received on the premises by staff, students, or members of the public
- Relationships with students

- ☐ Safety
- ☐ Sexual harassment
- ☐ Smoking
- ☐ Working under the influence of alcohol or illegal drugs or possessing them on campus

Policies and procedures for students could include, but may not be limited to:

- ☐ Academic dishonesty
- ☐ Attendance and absences
- ☐ Attending under the influence of alcohol or illegal drugs or possessing them on campus
- ☐ Compensation for massage prior to receiving a license, including tipping policy
- ☐ Dress code
- ☐ Ethics violations
- ☐ Grading
- ☐ Graduation
- ☐ Proof of liability insurance
- ☐ Reporting inappropriate behavior of a staff member, clinic client, or another student
- ☐ Reporting injuries received at school or while on a school-sponsored outing
- ☐ Satisfactory/unsatisfactory academic progress
- ☐ Sexual harassment
- ☐ Smoking
- ☐ Teacher/student relationships
- ☐ Timely completion of assignments
- ☐ Tuition and payments

Really, there are no situations too insignificant to warrant a policy and a procedure—as you'll find out the first time it arises and you're standing there wondering what to do about it. Your policies and procedures manual will be a living document that evolves over time. You may find new and better ways of handling things as you gain more experience as a school owner and employer.

Begin by stating your policy. For example:

Sexual Harassment

Policy: Sexual harassment will not be tolerated from any staff member or any student. Sexual harrassment is defined as unwanted sexual advances, including verbal and/or physical intimidation or coercion and/or requests for sexual favors. Any teasing, verbal commentary, unwelcome flirting, and unsolicited touching that creates an offensive or hostile environment will not be tolerated.

Procedure: Any student who has a complaint regarding sexual harassment from a staff or faculty member should report it immediately to the school owner, who will conduct an investigation by questioning both the complainant and the accused. A finding of sexual harassment on the part of a staff or faculty member will result in immediate termination. Any student who has a complaint regarding sexual harassment from a fellow student should report it immediately to the instructor, who will report it immediately to the owner. A finding of sexual harassment on the part of a student will result in termination of program participation and no refund will be given. If a student feels that a proper resolution has not been reached, a complaint may be filed with the state board of massage therapy.

Sound a little harsh? Yes, it does, but that's your prerogative. You may choose a less drastic measure, like one written warning before termination, but bear in mind that there is a lawsuit mentality prevailing in America. Your failure to terminate a teacher who is in fact sexually harassing students could result in a lawsuit against you and bad publicity for your school. When you're writing your policies and procedures, keep that in mind. Take a good look at each item as you're writing your manual and ask yourself these questions: Is it fair? Can I equally apply this to everyone? Is this policy illegal, immoral, or discriminatory in any way against any population? If it passes that litmus test, you have probably written a good policy and a good procedure.

Part II

School Records and Documentation

The biggest mistake regarding record keeping is not writing things down or not remembering where you wrote it down.
~David Mellam

Chapter 5

Document Everything

Attendance, grades, payments, injuries and incidents; basically, you need to document everything that goes on in your school, if it pertains to the education and/or safety of your students or the operation of your school as a business. In addition to the state board, the state revenue department and the IRS, you may have other entities to satisfy, such as an accrediting organization or a financial aid lender.

Keep in mind that the forms we have provided are just examples, and you may wish to make modifications to suit your own situation.

The most important consideration is that your documents should all be in agreement with each other. When you are adapting these forms for your use, or creating your own forms for documentation, proofread carefully to be sure that everything that should match does match. Your catalog, enrollment agreement, policies and procedures, and all printed matter related to those should be in perfect agreement in order to provide legal protection.

If you have decided to seek accreditation from COMTA or another entity for your massage school or program, bear one thing in mind: *if it isn't documented, it doesn't exist.*

The Application Process

The first document to consider is the application your school requires of potential students. Of course you have to gather the identifying information like name, address, education, etc., but how far do you wish to go beyond that? An application can be used to cut the wheat from the chaff at a very early stage. Bear in mind, public institutions such as community colleges are open to everyone...they can't legally turn people who might be unsuitable for the massage profession away. That's not the case with a privately owned school.

Some state boards require criminal record checks of all people entering health care professions and other licensed professions. if your state board does not require criminal record checks of applicants, it is your prerogative to do so at your school, and to have the policy that you will not admit those who have been convicted of a felony in *x* number of years, for example, or that you will not admit anyone who has ever been convicted of a sex crime or violent crime. If you choose to admit students with criminal records, but your state board does in fact have rules regarding applicants with criminal records, ethically you should state that in your catalog and on your enrollment agreement.

It's your right to make your application process as thorough as you want. You must require proof of graduation from high school or the equivalent. Don't just require it; look it over carefully. Keep in mind that the study of massage includes a lot of science: anatomy and physiology, pathology, kinesiology, ergonomics...while of course students can always improve themselves, the student who consistently failed every science class in high school is probably going to have a big struggle to learn the science accompanying the study of massage.

A community college I (Laura Allen) recently visited as a COMTA site reviewer had an admission policy in place regarding passing grades not only in massage sciences, but also in biology, algebra and English—fine if it was a second language—but that had to be proven by passing an ESL (English as a Second Language) exam. The school provided a remedial program for those that didn't make the cut, and anyone serious about getting into the massage therapy program was obligated to take it. That immediately increased their chances for success in the program. Realistically, algebra has nothing to do with massage and the lack of knowledge of it isn't going to keep anyone from being a good massage therapist—but the fact that the applicant has to jump through some hoops and expend real effort in order to make it into the program demonstrates dedication and determination.

You want your students to be set up for success, not set up to fail. You could require an entrance exam along with the requirement that a certain grade be met in order to allow enrollment. If a potential student fails it, then studies hard enough on their own to retake and pass, that shows true motivation to attend school. Some schools require applicants to write a substantial essay that is essentially a biography, and it must explain in detail why they want to enter massage school. That's a good tool for assessing motivation.

Whatever you decide to include as part of your application process, be sure to gather appropriate documentation to accompany the actual application. You may run a paperless school by scanning all documents, or keeping physical files, but either way, be sure to include the file checklist of necessary documents.

A sample basic application appears as Form 1 in Appendix I. An accompanying checklist of documentation to accompany the application appears as Form 2 in Appendix 1. A notice of deficiency in the application appears as Form 3 in Appendix I.

The Enrollment Agreement

Your enrollment agreement needs to be very detailed. Whatever actions and behaviors you expect from students must be spelled out; you can't depend on verbal rules to suffice. The intent is to have a binding document that protects you in the event a student claims not to have known that something is required or that something they have done is against the rules, for example. An example of an enrollment agreement appears as Form 4 in Appendix I.

Documenting Progress

Once the student begins their education, there will be numerous things that need documenting, such as attendance, hours spent in the student clinic, outside massages completed, internships completed satisfactorily, grades, and so forth.

Attendance

Some schools no longer take attendance, but instead grade on whether the student completes the work and performs in class and/or clinic. We urge taking attendance. If it isn't a requirement that students be physically present for *x* number of hours, they are going to miss a lot of information. Making up work is acceptable when necessary, but there's no substitute for class interaction and being there in the moment. A sample attendance form appears as Form 5 in Appendix I. A sample form for documenting makeup work appears as Form 6.

Practice in the Field

One of the greatest things for students is to receive apprenticeship-type training from successful professionals. Forging partnerships with local chiropractors, spas, and self-employed massage therapists can be a valuable part of the education process. It's important to vet the facilities and people you'll be sending your therapists to; don't just pull someone out of the phone book. Seek out businesses that have been in operation for at least several years and that have a professional image in the community. Again, a verbal agreement is not good enough. A sample contractual agreement for an externship appears as Form 7 in Appendix I. The primary purpose of field practice is to acclimate students to working in the real world, and part of that includes feedback from clients. A sample form for obtaining an evaluation of the student's work appears as Form 8 in Appendix I.

Another opportunity for on-the-job experience, as well as paying it forward, is to have a community service requirement as part of your educational program. A sample form for documenting community service appears as Form 9 in Appendix I.

Bear in mind that some states require a faculty member to be present for all organized student activities.

The Student Clinic

A student clinic serves several purposes:
- To introduce students to dealing with the public
- To familiarize students with the intake and interviewing process
- To give students the opportunity to get feedback from someone other than their instructors and classmates, facilitating skills in client communication
- To give students practical experience in writing SOAP or whichever form of progress notes are used in your school
- To expose students to as many different body types and personalities, different conditions, and different contraindications as possible
- To introduce massage therapy to the public in your area by offering free or low-cost massage

A sample student intake form appears as Form 10 in Appendix I. A sample client evaluation form for the student clinic appears as Form 11 in Appendix I. A sample student clinic sign-in form appears as Form 12 in Appendix I. A sample student SOAP note form appears as Form 13 in Appendix I.

A word to the wise: the purposes of a student clinic are listed above. The purpose of a student clinic is not to be a cash cow for the school. Some state boards have put a limit on the number of hours a school may require a student to work in the clinic for just that reason.

Staff and Faculty Documentation

The most important part of staff documentation is having adequate written job descriptions in place. The people you hire have the right to know what is expected of them, and it will save you the frustration of delegating tasks on a piecemeal basis if you make it clear from the outset of employment exactly who is to do what.

Appendix I contains sample job descriptions for the following positions:
- Form 14, Job Description for School Director
- Form 15, Job Description for Administrator
- Form 16, Job Description for Chief Financial Officer
- Form 17, Job Description for Lead Instructor
- Form 18, Job Description for Teaching Assistant
- Form 19, Job Description for Adjunct Instructor
- Form 20, Job Description for Externship Supervisor

Contracts

While it would be a nice gesture to hire people on a word and a handshake, it's not wise. A written contract should be on file for every person you hire. It should be attached to the job description, pointed to the policies and procedures manual, and should state that the employee agrees to perform the duties outlined there, in addition to the other important points of the agreement: salary, time off, cause for termination, notice expected, and any other points that are important to you. A sample contract appears as Form 21 in Appendix I.

Evaluation of Staff and Faculty

An evaluation of staff and faculty on an annual, biannual, or quarterly basis is a good idea. The larger your operation and the more people you employ, the more important it becomes. It might be easy to notice a deficiency in someone's work if you only have one staff member, but keeping track of multiple employees is a much bigger task.

When it comes to evaluating faculty, your opinion as the owner certainly counts, but student evaluations will tell the tale of how an instructor is doing. There's one complainer in every crowd, but if multiple students have the same criticism of a teacher, you should take heed of that.

Using written evaluations for all employees insures fairness in the process. The written evaluation should be congruent with the job description of the particular employee; you can't hold a person responsible for not having done a good job on something you haven't spelled out as a required responsibility. A sample written evaluation for a staff member appears as Form 22 in Appendix I. A sample student evaluation for faculty members appears as Form 23 in Appendix I, and a student evaluation summary for faculty members appears as Form 24. It is suggested that all three forms be used to evaluate faculty.

Administrative Records

Although strictly speaking, grades, transcripts, and release forms are student forms, it normally falls on the school administrator to compile and maintain those forms. The design of your particular student report card will depend on several factors: the length and divisions of your program, such as whether you're operating on the quarter system, semester system, or modular system and credit hours or clock hours; the type of grades you choose to use (numerical grade, letter grade, or pass/fail), and the types of classes you are teaching.

A sample student report card appears in Appendix I as Form 25. A sample transcript appears as Form 26. A sample student record release form appears as Form 27.

Accreditation

As stated at the beginning of this chapter, if you are seeking (or maintaining) accreditation from COMTA or another entity, documentation is required...if it isn't documented, it doesn't exist. COMTA is the only accrediting body devoted to the massage profession; other accrediting agencies bestow credentials on everything from airplane pilots to lawnmower repair schools. If you're going to seek accreditation, go for COMTA.

Gaining accreditation is expensive, time-consuming, and requires a lot of diligence. Accreditation also requires peer review of documentation and inspection of the physical facility. Since there are a lot of hoops to jump through on the road to accreditation, you may wonder "why bother?" Simply put, it's a hallmark of excellence. It's a way to say "We're going beyond what the state requires to prove that we have a superior school."

Part of the accreditation process is a very thorough self-study report. Schools must review their policies, their procedures, the way they conduct business, the education they provide. If it's not documented, it doesn't exist. Peer reviewers study their documentation before getting to the site, and then do an actual visit to the school. Every syllabus, every lesson plan, every piece of documentation related to their educational process and their business proceedings is reviewed. The curriculum needs to fall in line with the mission statement. The education offered must match the learning objectives that are stated. When the reviewers show up for the site visit, they basically review every piece of documentation the school claims to have, to make sure it actually exists and to make sure it does what it claims to be doing.

The accreditation doesn't just earn a nice label for the school. It provides a measure of protection to the student, as well. It assures that the school has definite policies on qualifications for insuring the competency of instructors, absenteeism, grading, following a carefully thought-out lesson plan, and much more. It assures that financial aid is being administered correctly and that student finances are carefully documented. It assures that there are policies on sexual harassment, and that instructors have to continually improve themselves with technical training and continuing education.

A COMTA school can't rest on their laurels. It's an ongoing process of maintaining the standards, and regular review. A school that is poorly managed isn't going to cut the mustard. It's safe to say there aren't any diploma mills or haphazardly run schools among the ranks.

COMTA standards are on the organization's website. Anyone can access them. We challenge every single school owner in the country to review them one at a time, and see how your school stacks up. Take the leap and apply for accreditation. When peer reviewers review your documentation and show up for a site visit, they're not there to thump you on the head for any shortcomings; they're there to help you come into compliance with the highest standards in the massage profession.

COMTA is also always seeking competent peer reviewers. The training to be a reviewer is also available on the website. Visit www.comta.org, and come to COMTA.

Part III

Teacher, Teach Thyself

The mediocre teacher tells. The good teacher explains. The superior teacher demonstrates. The great teacher inspires.
~William Arthur Ward

Chapter 6

The Basic Elements of Teaching

Pedagogy is the study of teaching, the process of teaching, and is often used to identify strategies of instruction. **Andragogy** refers to the specific discipline of teaching adult learners. *Andragogy* is frequently used in the context of the entire life experience of an adult and what has been learned and self-taught along the way, rather than what is just learned in the classroom. The most important thing you can learn at the outset of your teaching career is that it is a never-ending process of learning for *you*—from your students, from peers, from activities designed for professional development, such as continuing your own education, keeping current with research, and lessons from the school of hard knocks—invaluable on-the-job experience that textbooks can't prepare you for.

You may be handed a syllabus and a lesson plan, or you may be asked to write one. A **syllabus** is simply an outline and summary of topics to be covered during a class—a list of **learning objectives**. A syllabus usually contains pertinent details such as the instructor's name and contact information, important dates for the class such as exam dates and deadlines for turning in assignments, any required prerequisites, the grading policies of the class, required texts and other materials, and any rules of the class. Don't just hand it out; review it verbally in class on the first day of school. An example of a syllabus appears below:

Massage Therapy Section 100
The Business of Massage

Laura Allen

Education Offices, Suite 2

Phone: 828-288-3727

lauraallen@massage.edu

Office hours: 8:00-10:00 am MWF, or by appointment

Course Description

This course is an introduction to the business skills necessary to operate a massage therapy practice for those who desire to be proprietors; it will also be helpful to therapists who work as independent contractors and employees. The material covered will include writing a business plan, company structures, taxes, marketing strategies, comparing employment situations, insurance, record keeping, and planning for retirement.

Learning Objectives

At the conclusion of this course, you will be able to:

- ☐ Identify the components of a business plan, and be able to write a plan for starting a business of your own.

- ☐ Explain the differences in company structures, including the types of corporations and sole proprietorships.

- ☐ Identify the taxes associated with being self-employed and with alternate employment situations.

- ☐ Implement marketing strategies for growing your business.

- ☐ Explain the differences in being a proprietor, an independent contractor, and an employee.

- ☐ Identify the differences in insurance coverage necessary to the business owner, as well as the different types of insurance that a practitioner may have the opportunity to accept on behalf of clients.

- ☐ Identify different methods of record keeping and be able to choose the one that works best for you.

- ☐ Implement financial strategies for planning for your retirement.

Required Texts

Laura Allen, *A Massage Therapist's Guide to Business* (LWW, 2010).

Laura Allen, *One Year to a Successful Massage Therapy Practice* (LWW, 2008).

Both books are available on Amazon.com and most Internet booksellers, and are also available in the school bookstore.

Required Work

You will be required to write a business plan, which is due on Monday, November 17 (the last week of class). You are expected to answer the end-of-chapter questions from *A Massage Therapist's Guide to*

Business, for the chapter covered in class that week, and turn them in each Friday. A midterm exam will be given on October 1, and a final exam will be given on November 21.

Grading

Grading is on a numerical scale and will be influenced by the following: class attendance and participation, timely submission of assignments, performance on assignments, and performance on exams.

Business plan: 20%

Weekly assignments: 20%

Class attendance and participation: 20%

Exams: 40%.

Attendance

Attendance is expected at every class. Excused absences (illness, death in the family, personal emergency) must be documented, and any missed work must be made up within two weeks of the absence. Arrival after the class starts will result in 1 point taken off the final grade for each incident of tardiness. Excessive absences will result in points taken off the final grade at the teacher's discretion. If you have a personal problem necessitating absence, please discuss it with me before taking the time off from class.

The Lesson Plan

A lesson plan is the schedule detailing how the learning objectives that were stated on the syllabus are going to be met. An effective lesson plan will include elements of lecture, discussion, demonstration, practical application, learning activities, and assigned work. Lecture can be supplemented with videos and PowerPoint presentations. Learning activities are limited only by your creativity...everything from having students draw the muscles on each other with a grease pencil to using modeling clay to make anatomical structures can keep it interesting. Table 6.1 is a sample lesson plan.

Table 6-1. Sample lesson plan: Anatomy Class

Week beginning	Chapter	In-Class Activities	Homework Assignments	Notes
September 1	1	Lecture: Intro to Anatomy,	Read chapter, do questions	Ch 1 quiz on Friday

		terminology games		
September 8	2	PP on Body Systems	Read chapter, do questions	Ch 2 quiz on Friday
September 15	3	Field trip to "Bodies" exhibit	Read chapter, do questions, write summary of field trip experience	Ch 3 quiz on Friday

That's just a short sample. Depending on the length of your class, you may want to be more detailed. For example, the lesson plans submitted to the NCBTMB by Approved Providers of Continuing Education must include a time breakdown, such as the one below for a neuromuscular therapy class:

8:00-9:00 Lecture about various conditions helped by NMT
9:00-10:00 PowerPoint-trigger points
10:00-10:40 Demonstration of upper body techniques
10:40-11:00 Break
11:00-12:00 First exchange of upper body techniques
12:00-1:00 Lunch
1:00-2:00 Second exchange of upper body techniques
2:00-3:00 Demonstration of lower body techniques
3:00-3:20 Break
3:20-4:20 First exchange of lower body techniques
4:20-5:20 Second exchange of lower body techniques
5:20-5:30 Wrap-up, questions and answers

A few words to the wise: Humor goes a long way toward taking the stress off learning something new. The introduction of an occasional cartoon in a PowerPoint, or including funny anecdotes will make students laugh and diffuse stress for those students who are feeling nervous about absorbing the material.

An effective instructor also encourages plenty of classroom interaction and time for questions and answers. Never refuse to answer a question or act as if a student is asking a stupid question—there's no such thing as a stupid question. Avoid giving BS answers! If a student asks something you don't know the answer to, don't be ashamed to say you don't know, and look it up. One good strategy is for both the student and the instructor to look it up and discuss any differences at the next class. Better to look a little bit uninformed and honest that to give a room full of students a false answer.

Addendums

Don't hesitate to have an addendum along with the syllabus, because it will give you more leverage when students complain that something wasn't in the class outline. Having any extra rules in writing will help you enforce them, and all you have to do when something comes up is have them read the section that they violated. Always include the following: the instructor has the right to change anything in the addendum at any time.

However, be forewarned that the majority of states have licensure now, and the precedent has been set that *students must be subject to the rules that were in place when their education began.* You are legally putting your program at risk by changing rules or requirements in the middle of the student's education. For example, if the initial policy when the student started stated that tuition is a certain amount, you can't change that after the enrollment agreement is signed and charge the student more money for his education. If it is a change such as there was no official dress code when the student started, implementing something like "Students are prohibited from wearing open-toed shoes" in the middle of the semester can be done successfully by giving an adequate notice about when the new policy will take effect. Particularly when the change would cost a student money, such as having to buy scrubs when you didn't require that at the outset, ample notice must be given.

How to be a Great Teacher: Advice from the Trenches

We have hundreds of massage therapists from all over the country on our Facebook pages, including a lot of educators. We asked the question "What makes a great teacher?" Here are some of the best answers:

Myself and all nine of The VC instructors follow a strict policy to first demonstrate and then talk/lecture afterwards. It has been my experience that there is far too much cerebral 'transponderance' occuring in class yet what we need is the visceral, tactile and anatriptic more often. Also, most valuable for me, instead of 'answering' some of the more emotionally charged/multi faceted, spiritually ladened questions from students, I have learned to reverse the the direction and request that the student "to repeat the question to their soul today 108 times". Answers are like booby traps yet questions allow life to open and thrive with creativity and inspiration.
        ~Mukti Michael Buck

Be creative; make learning fun. Understand and know your student. Inspire them to learn. Stay on top of research and don't teach what you learned 20 years ago; it may not apply. Please don't just read from a book, be interactive with your students. Great teachers don't learn from a book - they learn from experience! Great teachers have passion and dedication and will always look for a way to support and help their student understand the material. They must listen to their students concerns. Teach them the 'reality' of the business!
~Gloria Coppola

As an instructor I am trying to uncover their own inner knowledge at the expense of not being "liked." Same philosophy I used as a parent.
~Taya Countryman

Be simple. Be clear. Be fair. Be Authentic.
~Karen Curran

Listen to Whitney Lowe. First is his near perfect cadence and tone. Second is his ability to explain the complex in understandable terms. That's my two cents.
~Scott Dartnall

A great teacher doesn't teach, but rather facilitates learning. It's all about the student.
~Earon Human Davis

Great teachers are always looking for ways to be better.
~Susie Davis

Know what you are teaching. This may mean that you have to continually study to stay up on everything you are teaching. This is not a bad thing. The best instructors do this because they love it and are always learning more. I have always said that "the body knows if the hands know the passwords". In teaching, the student knows if the teacher knows what they are teaching or are reading a manual. You might feel like you can go through the motions and follow a manual but, you won't be fooling anyone.
~Xerlan Deery

Being able to use my personal/professional experience to teach the students in the classroom the do's and don't of becoming a massage professional. I wish I had someone (teacher that is) that did that for me--it would've saved me a lot of time and energy.
~Shauna Flagg

You can only teach what you have attained. Otherwise you will be presenting material. Be congruent with what you teach. We teach by example, not by presentation of material.
    ~Barry Green

It's important to know how to draw the line between sharing your experiences--and your mistakes--and oversharing. Too often instructors overshare, or share inappropriate stories.
    ~Karen Hobson

I would like to see all teachers have certificates in Teaching Adult Learners. It's one thing to know our subject matter - it's another talent to know how to share that information in a way that people can actually learn. I required that of my teachers when I was running a school; they had to be at least enrolled in a course before I would hire them. And be scientific! Teach your students evidenced-based information. Get rid of the myths and stop passing them on to future generations.
    ~Lee Kalpin

A great teacher never forgets they are a student first, always expanding their knowledge and fine-tuning their abilities. Being a great teacher means you don't teach to a classroom; rather instructors have to learn to teach to individuals. A great teacher knows how to acclimate themselves for different learning speeds.
    ~Craig Knowles

Remember teaching is something you do with your whole self. It's not just an imparting of information or technique. You do it with your whole body, your voice, your eyes, your heart - it's a performing art as well as applied science. As Martin Buber says, "It is not the educational intention that is fruitful, but the meeting that is educationally fruitful." Meet your students on your common human ground.
    ~David Lauterstein

Something that took me a long time to learn: don't try to correct everything the student is doing wrong all the time. Give them some space to figure it out on their own. Otherwise it can be too discouraging.
    ~Alexei Levine

A great teacher must always remember that they once sat where their students are and should always respect that experience.
    ~Kenny Lyons

The best teaching advice I got from my teachers at school was to use the time in school to experiment. Experiment with types of lotions/oils, music, table height, etc.
~Lisa A. Mellers

It'a all about the student 'getting it.' What it takes to make the bulb light up is being able to convey the information for each learning style.
~Patricia J. Pape

Move around the classroom while teaching vs. standing still up front. It gives you the chance to connect with everyone.
~Lisa Santorini

Teaching is a skill you need to learn, just as massage therapy is a skill you need to learn. Be sure to include teacher education in your personal development plan.
~Jan Schwartz

It is not possible to know everything, but we should know what we are teaching. Review every lecture every time; things change and understanding evolves. Inspire, motivate and make it fun. Love what you do, it's infectious.
~Gail Selbie

I infuse humor into the class, especially when discussing "sensitive" subjects.... very clear information with a bit of humor infused helps them to remember while still having an appreciation for the seriousness.
~Ivy Jo Staton

Authenticity, inspiration, empathy and practice, practice, practice.
~Brian TeWater

(1) Teach with compassion and empathy. (2) Focus on the joy of serving. (3) Make every act a sacred act. (4) Practice active listening. (5) Encourage each student to be the best he or she can be. (6) Inspire your students to see their own essential magnificence. (7) Take time to teach mindfully. (8) Teach in a way that students can develop and enhance real life skills instead of teaching to the test. (9) Offer praise for accomplishments, no matter how small. (10) Feel genuine gratitude for the students in your life.
~Ariana Vincent

Bring in clinical scenarios from your practice, and link each story

directly to the learning objectives of the lesson or course. Know the tone you want to set at the beginning of each class, and set it. Breathe--early and often. Teach from different parts of the room, to include everyone. Get curious (not defensive) when challenged by a student. And that Goethe quotation, something about treating "people as if they were what they ought to be and you help them become what they are capable of being."
~Tracy Walton

Better than a thousand days of diligent study is one day with a great teacher.
~Japanese Proverb

Chapter 7

Classroom Management 101

Managing a learning environment is an exercise in multi-tasking. You have to manage paperwork and/or electronic documentation. You have to manage the students. You have to manage your schedule and your class instructional time, and the time you spend in your office. Somewhere in the midst of all that, you get to actually teach.

Developing skills in the management of *people* is the most important part of effective classroom management.

Attendance

Chances are there is a school-wide attendance policy in place, and it should be strictly enforced. Students who are chronically late or who habitually leave early disrupt the rest of the class. Penalizing offenders, and those who have excessive absenteeism, cuts the wheat from the chaff. Students who are serious about their massage education will make every effort to be present and on time, barring a genuine emergency. Give a small reward—even if it's just a certificate—for students with perfect attendance.

Chatty Kathy

There will always be a student that feels the need to talk as much as possible, which can disrupt the flow of the class. Sometimes a student keeps asking questions to the point that some of the other students become jealous, because you are spending more time catering to one student rather than sharing your knowledge in general. One effective strategy is to imagine you are being given an award and you can only give a five-word acceptance speech. Give your answer but make it as short as possible. Try this the next time you feel the need: once you answer the needy student's question, then ask other students if they have any questions; it will show them you want to know what they are thinking too. Asking random questions related to the day's lesson helps keep the class on topic.

Cliques

Having a clique is just like reliving high school. It's great that some students are friends in school, but it becomes a problem when people feel left out. It's not our job to make sure everyone gets along, but the more you can break the cliques up in the beginning, the better it will be in the long run. The best advice would be to have students pair up with different classmates each class. That way you will be sure that each student is experiencing the touch of different students and discourage those who seem determined to be joined together for the duration of the class.

Dress Code

If your school has a stated dress code policy, your obligation as a teacher is to model that and enforce it. Some schools have handled this by requiring scrubs, or khakis and polos. If the school is lacking a professional dress code, then you should model professional dress anyway. If it isn't spelled out in the school's rules, you may not be able to penalize the student who comes to the clinic dressed in cutoffs and flip-flops. The burden will be on you to be sure that your students are taught what constitutes dressing in a professional manner—so don't *you* show up in cutoffs and flip-flops.

Favoritism

It's hard sometimes to share all your attention with all the students equally. Your ease—or difficulties—in managing students has everything to do with the relationships you establish with them at the outset. You're not here to make friends.

You want the students to like you, but keep in mind that being friends with them outside of class is a dual relationship that can cause problems. Once other students finds out an instructor is friends with one of their classmates, they can start to feel jealousy and resentment. We all have favorite students—but the other students should never know that.

If you constantly praise certain students or call on your favorites all the time in class, other students will think they are not as good as the praised student. It's important to try and balance positive praise with constructive criticism. If you put too much emphasis on positives, then they won't be prepared for the real world, because they think they don't need to improve on anything. If you are always giving out criticism, then they will start lacking the confidence. Find the middle ground.

Be firm and consistent with your rules and your treatment of all students. What you enforce with one must be enforced with all. You can't let your favorite student slide for being late if you don't let the most troublesome student in the class do the same.

Know it All

In every class, you will run into students that think they know everything and they will test you whenever they get a chance. They aren't necessarily bad students, but that is how some people are wired. Instead of buying into confrontation that will just build a big grudge between you and the student, ask them how they came up with that knowledge; let them share it with the class, and then ask them to think of a different option or opinion on the topic. It helps them think even more and see other sides to it.

Phones

You are guaranteed to have cell phones go off in class and before you get all frustrated, you can let them know your rules the first day.

Laura Allen's rule: All cell phones must be set on vibrate, period. One reminder given at the beginning of class should be sufficient.

Ryan Hoyme's rule: If a cell phone rings in class, the guilty party has to bring food for all the students in that class, the next class period. It has worked out great and another student confessed to me after graduating massage school that he called other students' phones in class, just to get food the next class period. My rule about cell phones in the clinic is if a student's cell phone goes off while giving a massage to the public, then they have to give that client another massage on their own time for free. You will always get a student that says they need to leave their cell phone on, because they are expecting an important call and I tell them that is fine, but they still have to bring in food the next class for everyone. They sometimes decide the call isn't that important after all.

Rule Breakers

It's your job to enforce the rules of the school and your classroom. If you don't enforce them, then the students that abide by the rules will get upset and start to complain. The more you let things slide, the less the rule-breaking students will respect you.

Students Gossiping About Other Students

You need to stop this as soon as you hear it. Not only is it unprofessional, which should be stressed, but also because in a small classroom setting, those comments can come back to the person being gossiped about very quickly. That results in hurt feelings and tension in the classroom. Ask the instigator if it's something they would say to the student's face and point out if they say no, that they shouldn't be saying it to anyone.

Students with Special Needs

Some of your students will have learning or physical disabilities. It's necessary to have documentation in their file and note what steps you have taken in order to accommodate them. Students with disabilities may require special consideration; for example, a blind person may be given tests orally, or a hearing-impaired person may be allowed to bring a sign-language interpreter to class. The Americans with Disabilities Act prohibits discrimination against any person who has disabilities, and that is particularly true for any school that participates in Title IV financial aid programs.

Pearson Vue, the testing agency that administers the licensing and certification exams for both the Federation of State Massage Therapy Boards and the National Certification Board of Therapeutic Massage & Bodywork, will make special accommodations for disabled students.

Study Groups

Encourage students to start a study group at regular times of the week. It works out great, if you can find a time when most of them can meet. Since many adult learners also have jobs, it will have to be a mutually agreed-upon time that suits the majority. Each quarter/semester/module have them revisit it. It's very important to have the students that are in the same class try to study together, so they are all focused on the same material.

Trauma and Drama: The Troubled Student

It's a standard practice in new classes to have the students go around and introduce themselves and share a little about themselves. Some students will share what others may think is inappropriate information or be too personal with people they're meeting for the first time. Particularly in smaller classes, students tend to share too much and it's hard to control that when you aren't around.

Having a student that is having family problems or relationship problems can affect other students and the dynamics of the entire classroom, if that student can't control their frustrations. Sometimes it may be necessary to talk to them outside the classroom to explain to them that their constant dumping of their personal problems is making it hard for the other students to keep focused on the class. You may sometimes have to remember—and remind the student—that we are not mental health counselors, and if they need more help, that you know where to refer them to.

Definitely (but gently) remind them that if they are in the habit of talking about their personal problems to everyone in class, they are apt to do the same with clients, and it needs to be ingrained in them now that doing so is unacceptble behavior in a therapeutic relationship. Remind them that massage therapists are there to take care of their clients, and when we start sharing our personal woes with them, clients can be made to feel like they should be taking care of us.

The Other Instructor Does it This Way

Assuming you're not teaching the entire curriculum, you may be caught in the middle with students saying their other instructor does it this way or says so-and-so, and why don't you?

Ego doesn't have a place in massage. There is no one way that's the right way. You can get this across to students by answering "I usually perform it this way, but there are many different ways and the more you learn, the better off you are." Remind your students that they will learn just a portion of what they need to know in class, and the real learning starts when they actually start practicing. Never put down the other instructor's methods. If you don't agree with how the other instructor is doing something, make sure you never vocalize it with the students and talk to the instructor when the students are not around about it.

If an instructor is perpetuating something about massage that you know not to be true—those pesky old "myths of massage" that keep hanging around—like our old favorite, "massage causes you to detox," print out the research disproving their point of view and present them with it. Use a credible source like PubMed or a peer-reviewed journal.

One way to avoid this situation is by having regular faculty meetings, particularly at the beginning of the program and whenever new faculty comes on board. Discussing curriculum and bringing potential problems to the forefront before they happen is the best course of action.

More on the Myths of Massage

We just can't leave this part out. Don't **you** be the one guilty of perpetuating the myths of massage. Here is a list of the most common ones that just keep going around:

- **Massage causes you to detox.** We're repeating this because it is probably the most prevalent myth. A) The word "toxin" is misused all the time. Metabolic wastes and toxins are two different things. A toxin is a poison substance introduced into the body, such as a snake bite, or chemotherapy. Metabolic wastes occur naturally, and they will leave the body through the digestive system, the urinary system, and the integumentary system whether a person receives a massage or not.
  B) Assuming anyone actually *has* toxins in their body, we can't squeeze them out with a massage, no matter how much we'd like to.
- **Massaging your breasts prevents breast cancer.** Other than the fact that you are more apt to discover a lump in the breast by giving yourself frequent massage, there is no evidence to support this.
- **You shouldn't massage people who have cancer.** The vast majority of cancer patients can safely receive massage. Ask any cancer patient to get a release from their doctor before receiving massage; if there's any reason not to massage, they'll let you know it.
- **Any good massage should leave you feeling sore the next day (otherwise known as no pain, no gain).** Hogwash, plain and simple. While deep work may leave the client feeling sore, a massage doesn't have to be deep in order to be effective, nor does it necessarily have to leave the client feeling sore. Some people have more tolerance than others for deep work. The diligent thing to do is inform clients, particularly those who have never had a massage, that they may feel sore, but it isn't a given.
- **You shouldn't massage pregnant women in the first trimester.** Again, there is no research to support this. If a woman has a problem pregnancy, then there may be valid reasons not to give her a massage, but under normal circumstances, it's just another myth. Do women stop working, exercising, and having sex during their first trimester? Normally,

no, they don't. Generally, massage is perfectly safe during the first trimester. If there is any doubt, get a release from the obstetrician. Along with this one is the myth that massaging a pregnant woman's feet and ankles will cause a miscarriage. There has never been any evidence presented to support this claim.

- **Massage gets rid of cellulite.** Please, folks. If that was the case, every woman in America would be lining up to get one, and frequently. There is no research to support this. Of course, there are some products being sold to and used by massage therapists making this claim, and again, if the only research appears on the product's website and was not conducted by an impartial third party, enough said.

- **Massage flushes lactic acid out of the muscles.** In fact, research has been published to the contrary—that massage actually prohibits lactic acid from leaving the muscles. Along with this is the myth that lactic acid is responsible for muscle soreness, another claim without any basis in reality.

These are just a few of our favorites, and there are plenty more where they came from. A good rule of thumb: Don't say "research shows" unless you can show the research. And recognize that one study is not proof of something, even when it's a valid, peer-reviewed study. Research is meant to be replicated.

Chapter 8

Tips for Teaching

Adult Learners

While some students may come to massage school straight out of high school, many are older people who wish to make a career change. It's a challenge to teach people who may span ages from 18 to 70.

It's important to remember that adult learners may be many years removed from the educational environment, in need of an adjustment period for just getting into the flow of returning to school, and a refresher in good study habits. Adult learners bring maturity, established viewpoints, their pre-conceived notions and experiences to the classroom, and are often the most highly motivated students, usually juggling home and work so they can get training to make a career switch.

Activities for Learning

Keep it interesting by mixing it up! Add some fun exercises to your lectures and PowerPoint presentations. You're probably incorporating the obvious tools into your classroom: a skeletal, muscle, and other models that can be used for labeling activities, charts and flashcards for quizzing, but don't overlook the not so obvious. For example, have your students draw the muscles or trigger points on each other using china markers. Have them make an anatomical structure using Play-Doh, or study movement and structural relationship using a tensegrity model. It will make study time seem like play time.

Alumni

Your past graduates can be a great resource for your classroom. Successful graduates can be great motivators for your students. Host an Alumni Day annually so former students can come and interact with your class. Keep in touch with e-mail newsletters and invite graduates to the school clinic, or to be a demo person in a hands-on class. Encourage alumni as mentors. Some may even be future employers of your present students. It's a win-win relationship to maintain.

Ancillaries

Most good textbooks these days have accompanying ancillary

materials for instructors, including lesson plans, ready-made PowerPoints, question banks, and other resources. Don't take up all your time reinventing the wheel! If you (or your school, if it's not your personal decision of which book to use) are still using textbooks without good ancillaries, switch. The ancillaries are usually prepared by the author—who obviously knows the material very well—and will be great time savers.

Assignments

Assigning too much homework or no homework can be a bad thing, so how much should you assign? 30-60 minutes a week per class is sufficient. If you break down the assignments into sections, then it won't overwhelm the students as much. Give ample time for research paper assignments. A good homework strategy is having them summarize the weekly chapters *prior to* discussing it in class. You can assess if they understand what they have read and get more feedback about that chapter.

Avoid Teaching Too Much

Avoid the temptation to keep giving your students information. If you try to pack everything you know into their training, they'll be suffering from information overload. And most importantly—they need to learn some of it for themselves.

Be Prepared

If you've ever attended a class where the teacher didn't seem well prepared, you know it's not an ideal experience. Teachers are human, after all, and there will be a day when you're running late or frazzled by some incident, and you just don't have it together. So do have it together—every day. Before leaving the classroom for the day, have everything in place you need for the next day.

It's an undeniable fact that all instructors, whether they're teaching kindergarten or massage, spend a lot of their own (unpaid) time away from the classroom preparing for school. You don't want to take up your whole weekend with classroom preparations, or be glued to the task every night after dinner when you should be enjoying family or personal time, either. Set a schedule for yourself for preparing, and stick to it.

At the end of each day, enroll the students in cleaning up after themselves, putting away the classroom supplies that have been used, and getting their massage tables or other items prepared for the next day. Point out that this is good preparation for their entry into the working world, where they'll have to perform these tasks every day.

Community Service

Having the students being involved in community service would help them relate to what is going on out in the real world. Have them pick one charity or needy population, such as people in homeless shelters or abused women's shelters they want to help with their newly found skills. Providing massage to an underserved population is rewarding for the giver as well as the receiver. In some student massage clinics, a portion of the proceeds may be given to a charity. If it's an organized community event involving more than one student, as opposed to an individual project, bear in mind that a faculty member may need to be present to supervise.

Constructive Criticism

Get the message to your students that constructive criticism is a good thing, and that the point is not to make them feel bad but to help them learn from their mistakes. For every massage they give to the public, it would be a great idea to have the client fill out a feedback form. Tell the students to date the feedback form and periodically look at them and make sure they don't do the same mistake twice. Go over them with the student to explain more in depth of what they should do differently.

It's important for students to be encouraged to give each other real feedback. Instead of just saying "that was great," get them in the habit of saying "That was good, here's a suggestion to make it better."

Employers

Cultivating relationships with area employers serves several purposes for you and your students. Chiropractors, spa and salon managers, rehab clinic managers, hotel and resort human resource managers are all possibilities as future employers of your graduates. First, you'd like for them to know that you are graduating knowledgeable and quality students from your program. Second, they can partner with you in several ways. Have a future employer as a guest speaker (vet them first). Ask if some of them would be willing to conduct mock job interviews with the students for the purpose of giving them constructive criticism about their answers and general demeanor during the interview. Some may be able to provide externship opportunities for on-the-job training, or serve on an advisory board for your students. You might host a career fair and invite potential employers to the school on the same day near the time of graduation.

Feedback

Ask the students for feedback about how the class is going a few weeks after beginning, in the middle and close to the end of it. Try not to make it into a complaining session, because you need to cover all that is on the syllabi and you really want to see how well they comprehend the information you are giving them. Handing out anonymous class evaluations can be very telling; some students might hesitate to tell the instructor about their complaints if they feel the individual is too sensitive to criticism. The point is to make the class better, so don't take suggestions for improvement as a personal attack on your teaching methods.

Field trips

Most students love field trips. Field trips can break up the monotony of the classroom, and are great for the students that are more introverted, because it gets them out in the community and helps them to socialize more. Some ideas for field trips are community service trips to do hand and foot massage for residents in nursing homes, or doing chair massage for emergency responders, nurses, or any deserving population. If you are located near a teaching hospital, you might arrange for students to observe a rotator cuff surgery (in a glass-enclosed theater, not in the actual operating room). The "Bodies" exhibit has been traveling the country for several years; that's a great one.

Games in the Classroom

Games are a great way to break the ice and to get the students to work together. Using Jeopardy games will get them to think more, while having a lot of fun. Having the students write questions to contribute to the game is a great strategy, but make sure they give you the questions a few days before the class so you can check the answers. You can have them make multiple choice questions but have them give you the references for the information, so you can make sure the answers are correct before asking them in class.

Gifted Students

Sometimes you will have students that you are so proud of, who latch on to every word or technique you give them. It's important not to use them as an example in your classes, but to have them help the students that are having a hard time. Sometimes gifted students know that they're gifted and it will make it harder for them to find a job, because they know they are good and they want to wait for that perfect job. It's your responsibility to let them know that they need as much experience as possible, so they can find the perfect job down the road. Avoid the urge to make the gifted students into the "teacher's pet." It will create resentment among your other students.

Grading

Some accreditation agencies or state boards may not allow Pass/Fail grading. It's an all or nothing type of grading that often doesn't suit students, either. Most want to do well and a letter or number grade shows that better.

Percentage grading is what a lot of teachers use, because it's easier to keep track of their grades and you just have to do a little division to find out the percentage and then you turn it into a letter grade.

A percentage grade looks like this:

90%-100% A
80%-89% B
70%-79% C
60%-69% D

Below 60%, F

A well thought out grading system is not just based on the student's test scores, but will also take into account completion of homework and class assignments, clinic attendance and performance, and overall participation in the class. Using a **rubric** for grading purposes will make the whole process less subjective. Rubrics specify the level of performance expected for several levels of quality. These levels of quality may be written as different ratings (e.g., Excellent, Good, Needs Improvement) or as numerical scores (e.g., 4, 3, 2, 1) which are then added up to form a total score which then is associated with a grade (e.g., A, B, C, etc).

Guest Speakers

Guest speakers are a great way to enforce what you are teaching and to give students the benefit of knowledge and experience of others who are successful in the healing arts. A chiropractor, spa owner, or past student who is doing well will make good guests. Ask them to include some stories about any difficulties they might have had when they first started in business, in the interest of giving students a reality check. Have each student write 5 questions they can ask the guest, so it will get the conversation going. Some speakers are better than others, so vet them first; a short interview where you are asking them questions that students might potentially ask is one way to see how responsive and articulate they're going to be.

Lab Time

Having open lab hours for the students to practice on each other (separate from student clinic, where they're working on the public) on their own time is a good idea.

Give the students some free time to practice their skills in lab in the interest of retaining what they've learned. It might be a few days before they practice that technique again and they will have lost the flow of it or even forgotten the technique all together. Be present during lab to offer suggestions and answer questions, but remember that the purpose of a lab is the practical application of what the student has learned, so avoid turning it into a continuation of the classroom lecture.

Try to bring in senior students or professional massage therapists into the student lab each quarter/semester. They tend to give better feedback and pointers that will help your newbies learn better. Don't forget to encourage your students to come back and participate when they become practicing therapists.

Media in the Classroom

Youtube is a great way to bring media into the classroom. You can have your students view a view clip on massage and them have them make comments afterwards. Another option is the use of PowerPoint presentations, but try not to have all your lectures have long and boring PowerPoint slides. Add videos into your PowerPoints. It will give you a little break from lecturing. You can talk until you are blue in your face and not get your point across, but if someone else says it, then it can reinforce what you just said.

Another great use of media is to videotape your students for 5 minutes each while they are giving a massage. It would help them see their massage technique and their body mechanics from a whole new viewpoint. You could point out their ergonomics and see how well they flow with the massage. Athletes constantly look at all their past games to see what they can do differently and also to see the people they will be playing against. Seeing how other therapists deal with different situations will help each student become a better therapist.

Mentors

Encourage your students to find a mentor. You might keep a list of graduates who are now experienced therapists who will be willing to serve as mentors for your students. Many schools offer the opportunity to former graduates to host students for internships or simply have them arrange to receive a professional massage from a graduate, or to have the student give a massage to the graduate for critiquing purposes. Vet the graduates before recommending them as mentors. You want to know that they are conducting an ethical and successful business before sending your students to them.

Another great option is peer-to-peer mentoring. Pair up students that have certain weaknesses with others that excel in the areas they are lacking. You really have to know your students in order to do this effectively, and usually after 6-12 weeks, their true personalities start to come out, so that is when you may decide who to pair up with whom. Have the students fill out a feedback form after each session, so they can learn from it right away.

Don't forget to have your own mentor. Finding a more experienced teacher that you can turn to for support and guidance is one of the most important things you can do for your own career.

Plagiarism

The more you educate students about plagiarism, the more it cuts down on the problem. Particularly in this Internet age, students have often been guilty of cutting and pasting—sometimes an article or paper in its entirety—and turning it in as their own work. It's your job to check for plagiarism. If they keep getting away with it, some students will keep doing it, because it makes their homework load less. Every school has their own rules, and many will have you submit the plagiarized work to the education director or the director of the school, and they can give you the best options for the next course of action to follow.

There are websites that will help you find plagiarized work; often just googling a few sentences can help you find plagiarized work, too. It's important to review this with students on the first day of class so they're clear on expectations. It's a good thing to include the plagiarism policy on the syllabus so there's no excuse for a student to claim ignorance.

A word to this wise: you have to model academic honesty. Copying handouts from textbooks that you haven't adopted or the work of other teachers from classes you may have attended, using them for your own class and not crediting sources are two issues that we've seen many times. If you present someone else's work as your own, you're handing your students the notion that it's acceptable for them to do the same. Many publishers and/or authors will grant you permission to use their work for educational purposes for the asking—so don't fail to ask.

Pop Quizzes

Having an oral exercise with a few exam questions in each class will help students get used to answering questions under pressure—just like they'll be doing when they sit for a licensing exam. Pop quizzes can also be a handy tool for dealing with students who are chronically tardy or who leave early. The first day of class, announce that pop quizzes will be regularly given at the beginning or end of class, cannot be made up, and will account for x percentage of the final grade.

Require Students to Receive Professional Massage

As an assignment in their first class, require students to receive a massage from a professional massage therapist. Keep in mind that the fee should be mentioned in the finance section of the student catalog, if it is a required expenditure.

Ask the students not to tell the therapist that they are going to massage school, and have them fill out a questionnaire of mostly yes and no answers regarding what they learned about the massage. Some students may have negative comments about the massages they receive, so tell them it's better to have a massage you don't like in the beginning of your career, so you can learn what not to do. If you have them get their massages at the end of their first techniques class, they'll have an idea of what to expect, particularly if they have never had a professional massage before.

Some schools stipulate that students must receive a couple of professional massages before they even enroll into massage school, but if that isn't the case at your school, do incorporate it into the curriculum as a homework assignment.

Research in the Classroom

Teaching research literacy unfortunately has not been a priority at many massage schools. It is the *responsibility* of every instructor to teach research literacy in the classroom. Don't panic! That doesn't mean you have to teach elementary statistics or how to conduct a double-blind study. It does, at a minimum, mean that you should teach what constitutes valid research, and where students can find it. Unless it is a peer-reviewed journal, magazines usually are not good sources, unless the article contains valid research references. Teach your students what a credible source is. Impress upon them that finding undocumented and unreferenced statements on a massage website doesn't cut it. Practitioners are often guilty of putting unfounded statements on their own sites.

PubMed is a good starting point for locating research concerning massage therapy. The Massage Therapy Foundation is another good resource, especially the toolbar available on their website, which will help keep you up to date on current developments. The Touch Research Institute at the University of Miami Medical School has conducted a lot of massage therapy research, but their groups of subjects tend to be very small, and the studies are more suitable as pilot studies demonstrating evidence that further research should be conducted in a specific area.

Give students an education about Internet research. Remind them that any time they are researching a massage or other health-related product, for example, that any research appearing on a website where the product is being sold is going to be in favor of the product. Remind them to look for impartial third-party research that has no vested interest in the sales of the product.

Your students will also need to be reminded to credit sources. This goes back to the section on plagiarism; some students may not have the intention to steal another person's work, but they may be ignorant of the need and the way to credit sources, particularly Internet sources, if they're older students who lack experience in Internet research.

Social Media in the Classroom

Younger students have grown up using technology, and as a teacher, you need to understand as much about it as possible. You don't have to be an expert, but you should understand the terminology. Teaching a business class without covering social media is not doing a good service to your students. For an interesting class period, have a student or two teach everyone in the classroom about how to use Facebook, Twitter, LinkedIn, and other social media. Follow up with a brainstorming session of how to use what they have already learned in the business class and adapt it to the online world.

Create a "Group" page for your students on FB, and a fan page for your school and/or student clinic.

Another good exercise is to have the students review the FB pages of their classmates. Identifying yourself as a massage therapist—or massage therapy student—and having inappropriate pictures or content on your page is a bad idea, and one that students need to be reminded of. It's estimated that 80-90% of employers now check social media sites before hiring.

Student Clinic

A student clinic (open to the public, as opposed to the student lab) is a necessity for a massage school. Some schools handle this by having a clinic open daily, while some choose to do one day a month or something in the middle. It is vitally important, and in most places, the law, that a faculty member must be supervising the clinic at all times. In some states, it may be against the law to charge money in a student clinic. In others, there may be a stipulation that the school may keep the money but students are not allowed to receive any compensation. Be sure you are complying with the law in your state.

The student clinic is an opportunity to introduce your students to the community, and to get them used to dealing with the public, conducting intake interviews, and the other skills of taking care of clients.

When the public comes in to a student clinic, some of them tend to not give their full opinion; they don't want to seem critical of someone who is just learning. Some may have never had a professional massage before, so they don't have any experience for comparison's sake.

When clients don't give constructive criticism on the feedback forms, the students tend to have their egos boosted even more. It's great to have praise, but you need a balance while you are in school. Just recall how frustrated you were when starting out and dealing with clients that don't come in for regular massage, or those who don't come back at all. It's your job to prepare students for the frustrations and realities of massage, and to explain to them you can't please everyone.

Continuing Education

Talk to your students about continuing education while they're still in school. Most states require it in order to renew a massage license, and of course there are some who would take it whether it was required or not. Encourage them to look for classes that are actually appealing to them, as opposed to the closest or cheapest or most convenient thing. Encourage them to seek out continuing education that will inspire them, and that will teach them new knowledge, skills and abilities to bring back to their practice.

Chapter 9

Teaching Online

Distance education, or e-learning, as it is often called, is the fastest growing segment of education. While distance learning has been popular among continuing education providers for years, it is now also coming into more popular usage in entry-level massage programs. The National Certification Board for Therapeutic Massage & Bodywork changed their policies several years ago to allow up to 300 of the 500 hours of entry-level education required to sit for the certification exam to be distance learning. Be aware, however, that some states still do not accept distance learning for entry-level licensing; some boards have adopted rules specific to distance learning for both entry-level and continuing education, so be sure to check the practice act and guidelines for your state before assuming that distance learning is acceptable before proceeding.

Teaching online not only requires a certain amount of computer and Internet literacy over and above basic computer skills; there are other considerations as well. Depending on the format of the class, you may be conducting webinars, communicating through message boards, posting and receiving assignments through shared folders or public forums, chatting live, streaming video, or any combination of the above. Make sure you practice, practice, practice, and that as the teacher, you know what you are doing before the actual class or presentation.

The Benefits of Online Learning

To the student, the most obvious benefit of online learning is the convenience. Classes can be accessed from anywhere there's Internet service. The ability to check in to post assignments, watch videos, and communicate with classmates at any time is a real benefit to learners who have other work or family responsibilities. Online classes tend to be less expensive than their in-person counterparts. Another benefit is that students who need time to think before they respond can do that easily online. Shy students have the tendency to interact more on discussion boards than they do in a classroom, simply because it's required.

There's the convenience factor for instructors, as well. You can conduct a webinar or post assignments while you're at home in your pajamas.

You may post a semester's worth of work at one time, and then just check in on a regular daily or weekly schedule to respond to questions.

The Challenges of Online Learning

One of the biggest challenges for the student of online learning is cultivating self-discipline to keep current with the work. Particularly if the class is more open-ended and strict deadlines are not enforced for completion of certain tasks, or for checking in and posting at required intervals, you may find that students are not as diligent about adhering to a regular schedule as they would be if their physical attendance at the class was required. Some students may wait until the last minute and complete all the required work at once. While that may not be a big deal to a continuing education provider, it's more important in entry-level massage education to keep the students on a disciplined schedule. Do that by requiring at least one original posting per week, or x amount of comments on a fellow classmate's postings. As long as there's a deadline—and any penalty, such as a grade or attendance penalty for failing to meet it—you're doing what you can to make it a fair learning experience for all.

The same burden is on you. Some students have had the unfortunate experience of taking online classes where the teacher was the guilty party in failing to be a timely communicator. I (Laura Allen) had such an experience with an online course. The teacher would make an assignment, and then she would be several days late in posting any responses. She would invariably sign on to the forum with an excuse like "Sorry I'm a few days late...husband had a business trip, kids were sick..." While we can all sympathize with that, it's just as unprofessional to keep students waiting in an e-learning environment as it would be to skip classes or show up late if you were teaching a live class. Keep in mind that you are setting the tone for the class and you should model the behavior and timely actions you want everyone attending to have.

Another challenge in online learning can be the lack of verbal communication and the ability to read the body language, hear the tone of voice, etc., of the people you're interacting with.

Education and Training Solutions is an online education company owned by Jan Schwartz and Whitney Lowe, two well-known and well-respected massage therapists and educators. Judith McDaniel, an attorney, civil rights activist, and university professor, teaches the teacher training course. One of their class offerings is a class in how to teach effectively online. I (Laura Allen) was one of the first people to take it, and I would highly recommend it to anyone who intends to conduct Internet classes.

I've been told I'm quite entertaining in person...when I took the online course, I quickly found out that what works in person doesn't necessarily work online! Due to that lack of up-close and personal interaction, what might sound funny in person comes across as sounding sarcastic in cyberspace. It's doubly important, in online learning, to use language that is neutral and non-judgmental.

It's okay to use an occasional emoticon on an online forum, but avoid the overuse syndrome associated with emoticons and cyber-speak. Remember that you're conducting a professional class and leave off the OMG's and other abbreviations and all but the occasional emoticon.

Moderate and Facilitate

Part of your job as an online instructor will turn out to be that of a moderator. It often goes back to the issue of not being able to hear tone of voice and read body language, but online discussions can sometimes turn into snark-fests or heated arguments. Lay out ground rules at the beginning of the class that everyone should be respectful of the opinions of others, and that no personal attacks or bad behavior will be tolerated. You may need to give your students a refresher about civil discourse—the ability to argue intelligently and without malice—and a reminder about Internet etiquette; for example, to use more neutral language in online postings, and avoid the use of all caps, bold letters, and cyber-jargon.

Online students may need the occasional (or frequent!) reminders to stay on topic. Just like a Facebook thread, people will sometimes go off on a tangent that has nothing to do with the assigned topic at hand, and you have to rope them back in, just like you would in a live class.

Chapter 10

Becoming a Provider of Continuing Education

At this point in time, the National Certification Board for Therapeutic Massage & Bodywork is the usual go-to entity for becoming approved as a provider of continuing education. There are also a number of states that have their own approval requirements for providers. The best thing to do is check on the state board website of the state you'd like to teach in to find out if you need to apply directly with the state. A few that immediately come to mind are Florida, Texas, Alabama, Louisiana, and New York. New York is actually a special circumstance; they do accept continuing education offered by providers who are approved by the NCBTMB, with the caveat that any hands-on demonstration must be performed by a massage therapist licensed in the state of New York, and there is some additional paperwork required as well. Contact information for all the state boards appears in Appendix II.

The application to become an Approved Provider under the NCBTMB is available on their website at
http://www.ncbtmb.org/ceproviders_forms.php

The application may look long and daunting—but you should take heart. It's actually about half as long as it was a decade ago! The process has become more streamlined over the years, and hopefully by the time this goes to print, it will be entirely online.

In addition to giving contact information, the primary things on the application are stating learning objectives for your class, stating what category it falls into (ethics, deep tissue techniques, spa treatments, etc.), a time breakdown of lecture/discussion/demonstration/practice, and the lesson plan for how you're going to accomplish those objectives.

Just like the lesson plan for an entry-level class, the learning objectives need to be stated in measureable terms like the following:

At the conclusion of this class, the student will be able to (explain, demonstrate, define) _____ .

Avoid using general terms like "the student will *know*." The lesson plan should be constructed to match the learning objectives.

Documentation

Part of becoming a provider of continuing education is your commitment to good recordkeeping. There are templates for all the forms you need included in the handbook that accompanies the application on the NCBTMB's website. Sign-in sheets, transcripts, certificates of completion and achievement (certificates of achievement are given only in the event that a test is required proving that the student learned the material you presented), and class evaluations are required. You are obligated to maintain NCBTMB records for a period of four years.

Being Successful as a Provider

Providing continuing education is a very competitive market in most places these days. The key to success is in establishing yourself as a knowledgeable presenter who is also engaging and entertaining. You should be a subject matter expert in the subject(s) you are teaching.

Class evaluations are the best feedback you can get. They should be anonymous—don't require names—so that the person may feel free to give honest criticism.

There will always be complaints that the chairs were too hard, the room was too cold, and those kinds of things. Particularly if you're teaching in someone else's venue, those things may be beyond your control. But do take it to heart if you get more than one or two evaluations that say you weren't speaking loudly or clearly enough, or that the material was boring, and those kinds of things that we tend to take personally. You *should* take it personally...that doesn't mean to get upset over it, but if several people say you aren't speaking loudly enough, you probably aren't. Evaluations are a way for people to give both positive and negative feedback. Don't waste time feeling defensive about it, just fix the problem!

Integrity in Teaching

This has already been mentioned in this book, but it bears repeating. It's plagiarism to present someone else's work as your own. If you want to use portions of a published work, request permission. We've requested it ourselves plenty of times and never been turned down.

A former (former being the key word) colleague of ours attended a class in orthopedic massage presented by an internationally known teacher. He came home from the class, copied all the materials, put them together in a new handout, and immediately started teaching the class. He taught the class a couple of times and fizzled into oblivion. Some of the people who came to his class recognized the material as being right out of the other instructor's book and called him out on taking credit for it. One attendee even sent the handouts to the original author/educator. Just a little old-fashioned karma. Always, always, credit your sources any time you use something other than your own original thought to create a class.

Advertising Your Classes

A website is a given. If you're trying to establish yourself as an educational force, then get a professional-looking website, and have it set up for online registration. You want to make it as easy for the continuing ed consumer as possible.

The NCBTMB provides a free listing of all providers and what they are approved to teach—but not their classe schedules. They will also sell you all or part of their mailing list of nationally certified massage therapists to market to through direct mailing.

If you're a member of the American Massage Therapy Association, you may post classes on their website (www.amtamassage.org) at no charge. The same benefit is available to educators who are members of the Alliance for Massage Therapy Education (http://www.afmte.org/). There are numerous websites that cater to the massage therapy profession; some are free, some are fee-based, but there are plenty of places for you to post classes. They don't sell their mailing list per se—as in you don't get a copy of it—but for a fee comparable to buying a mailing list, the organization will do the mailing for you.

Most of the state AMTA chapters have newsletters that will sell you ad space, even though you may not be a member. Non-members are charged more for advertising, but it's still usually a good deal. Many chapters have a once-per-year issue that goes to all licensees in that state, not just their membership, so that can be an effective way to reach an audience. Some of the state massage boards will also sell their mailing lists.

Other options are the trade journals; those tend to be more expensive to advertise in—but they also reach a much wider audience.

Don't overlook social media. Facebook, LinkedIn, Twitter and other venues are free places to post your events, or you can pay for sponsored ads. Using Google AdWords can ramp up your attendance, if you use "pay-per-click" advertising.

Of course, you will want to cultivate your own mailing list. Collect e-mail addresses as part of your registration process, include an opt-out statement for those who don't wish to receive future mailings, and don't forget to market to those who have attended your classes before. When they appreciate what you have to offer, they come back—and give you good recommendations to others.

Chapter 11

The Best You Can Be: Reaching Your Full Potential

Like any other job, teaching has its highs and lows. There will be days when you feel satisfied with what you've accomplished, and days when you wonder why you do it at all. Most teachers aren't in it for the money; they're in it for the joy of teaching.

In order to be the best teacher you can be, the most important thing to realize is that your own education can never end. That's not meant as a reference to a continuing education requirement; that's just one piece of the puzzle.

The best teachers go beyond what is required, and they never stop learning. The people at the top of this profession are constantly attending classes and conferences in the quest to improve their skills and expand their knowledge. The day you feel like you know it all, do your students a favor—retire.

Training as a Teacher

Being handed a syllabus and a lesson plan doesn't make you a teacher anymore than being handed a rope makes you a cowboy. If you were an education major in college, or otherwise trained to teach, good for you. Having specific training in teaching adult learners is even better.

Hopefully, if you are hired to teach in a massage school, you will be provided with an orientation, at a minimum. If you are a massage therapist who is just starting to teach, the best things you can do—for yourself and for your students—is to take a teacher training class and to find an experienced instructor who will act as your mentor. Some state boards require that schools provide their instructors with adequate training in teaching methods, but in some cases it is vaguely worded and does nothing to spell out required content or expected knowledge and skills a massage educator should have.

There are not many programs or continuing education classes offered in teaching methods specifically for massage educators. The best-known one in the country is probably The Spirit of Learning®, started in 1998 by Carey Smith, co-director of Body Therapy Institute in Siler City, NC. Smith is the 2009 Jerome Perlinski Teacher of the Year and a 2011 inductee into the Massage Therapy Hall of Fame, and a pioneer who recognized the need for teacher training in the massage profession and created a 100-hour program.

Smith has recently expanded her program under the umbrella of the Center of Embodied Teacher Education, which includes a hand-picked corps of instructors who have studied with her. In addition to the 100-hour program, there is now an advanced mastery class for graduates of that program, a 3-day Teacher Bootcamp in core competencies and 1-day classes in different teaching skills are also available. An annual 2-day Graduate's Forum is also held for the purpose of sharing inspiration and building community among educators. An invitation-only apprenticeship program is also offered. As far as we know, it is the most comprehensive program currently available to massage therapy educators.

Smith and her husband, Rick Rosen, have both been instrumental in the advancement of massage therapy education for the past three decades. Rosen founded the Alliance for Massage Therapy Education and served as the first executive director, the last of many state and national offices he has held.

A listing of other teacher training programs offered by Approved Providers under the National Certification Board for Therapeutic Massage & Bodywork appears in Appendix V. Most of them qualify as continuing education for massage therapists as well, so if you're a teacher who is also a licensed therapist, you'll be helping yourself and getting credit for it as well. Please keep in mind that each state has their own continuing education requirements and may require individual state approval of providers.

The Personal Development Plan

Teachers in public schools are obligated to have a PDP—personal development plan—every year. It's a simple document detailing what it is they intend to accomplish in the way of self-improvement, and why and how they're going to do it. Massage school instructors and continuing education providers would do well to follow that example.

Foremost on your personal development plan should be keeping up with research and keeping your classroom materials updated to reflect current knowledge.

The evidence-informed practice of massage is the key to increasing the credibility of massage therapy and its integration into mainstream healthcare. Massage has been shown to be effective in the treatment of many conditions, and it's up to you to be informed of that so you can share it with your students, instead of repeating the myths of massage that persist. The Massage Therapy Foundation has a downloadable toolbar on their website that will help you keep in touch with the latest developments. A listing of other research resources for massage therapy appears in Appendix IV.

Most states do have a continuing education requirement for keeping your massage license, so make that a part of your plan. Don't view that as a burden; view it as an opportunity to get new information you can incorporate into your teaching methods, your classes, or your own practice of massage.

Your personal development plan may include workshops and conferences you want to attend, new books you want to read, online classes you want to take, new products you want to try. The list of things that can contribute to personal development is endless.

Having a written plan will bring you clarity and focus on what you want to accomplish. Defining *why* you are doing something will help keep you on task, particularly if there is something you need to do that you don't really enjoy, such as taking a particular class or attending a particular event.

The Personal Learning Network

Cultivating a personal learning network is easy to do. Start with your fellow instructors, if you're teaching in a massage school. It's a good thing to regularly come together to share information and discuss common problems. If your school is in an area large enough to support more than one massage school, consider inviting teachers from other schools to get together for networking purposes and to learn from each other. Don't wait on someone else to get the ball rolling. *You* be the one to start that group!

The two largest professional massage associations, ABMP and AMTA, both conduct school summits annually. Anyone from the education sector is welcome to attend. The Alliance for Massage Therapy Education also has an annual membership meeting. The authors have attended this meeting and found it to be a superior gathering of the best and brightest massage educators in the profession. All of these conferences serve the purpose of "educating the educators." Workshops and presentations include topics ranging from how to keep your massage school profitable, to research literacy, to teaching methods—much of the same information we're covering in this book— but hearing a variety of perspectives from top-notch educators is a singular experience that we encourage all teachers to avail themselves of.

Don't overlook social media. The Internet has made it easy to network with others. For example, Facebook has numerous group pages for teachers of massage therapy. There are groups for people who teach anatomy, business, and many other topics, and groups for teachers in general. It's a great way to share information with your peers all over the world. LinkedIn is another great business networking site with numerous groups for educators. Many well-known massage educators are on Twitter; subscribe to them and their posts will appear on your page whenever you sign in. ABMP has an online forum that's open to all; at any given time there are hundreds of groups and hundreds of discussions going on between the thousands of massage therapists on the site. POEM, the Project for Open Education in Massage is a community-supported, open-access resource providing educational materials, learning experiences, reference works, and interactive discussion for the massage profession. The Massage Learning Network is another great resource, where experts in the field have posted videos and are available to answer questions from students and practitioners.

Teacher Burnout

The first year of teaching is usually the hardest; you grow accustomed to the challenges, and you hit your stride. One of the difficulties in teaching is avoiding burnout. You want to remain fresh and excited about the job, and that's sometimes hard to do when you're teaching the same thing year after year. If you've been using the same lesson plan from one year to another, and not inserting new information into that, it's time to change that habit.

Over and above the benefits that your students receive from being research literate, as mentioned earlier, is the benefit to *you* of keeping current with the latest developments. Reading journals, searching PubMed, and keeping an eye on the Massage Therapy Foundation website for interesting case studies can help you keep in touch with what's going on in the world of massage therapy research. Add new information to your class as it becomes available. You owe it to your students.

We often preach the sermon of self-care to our students—and forget to do it ourselves. Everyone needs downtime and recreation; it's food for the soul. If you have to schedule your downtime, do it. And don't forget to schedule a regular massage. Even if you're getting massage from students, it's still good to go outside the school to visit a professional therapist. When you're on the table at school, you're still working, and it's not good to let every one of your own massage sessions be a student critique. Get some massage when you can just relax and enjoy it without worrying about evaluating the student.

Taking care of yourself is also modeling good behavior for your students. Remind them that if we're going to encourage clients to get regular massage, we should be doing it ourselves.

Good teachers are those who know how little they know.
Bad teachers are those who think they know
more than they don't know.
~R. Verdi

Appendices

Appendix I

Forms and Documentation

These forms may be downloaded so you may customize them for your school or classroom. E-mail a copy of your receipt to **Massagenerd@gmail.com** to receive the link to your download.

Form 1. Application for Admission to Massage School.

Last Name_____First_____Middle_____

Address_____ City

ST_____Zip Code_____Home Phone (   )

Cell Phone (   )_____Work Phone (   )_____

E-mail_____ Website_____

Current Employer_____Occupation_____

How long?_____Name of Reference_____

DOB _____Sex M_____ F_____ SS#_____

Emergency Contact_____Relationship_____

Phone #s Emergency Contact (   )_____

Highest Education Completed_____Institution_____Year_____

If you have any physical limitations and/or learning disabilities that will necessitate special accomodations during your education here please list details and special needs:

_____
_____

Do you hold any professional licenses in this or other states? Yes_____ No_____

If so, state, license and #_____Exp_____

Active Military Yes____ No____ Veteran _____ Branch of service_____

Are you applying for financial aid?

Have you been convicted of a crime, other than a minor traffic violation? Yes____No____

A copy of your criminal record must be provided to the school. If the answer to the above question was Yes, please attach a letter of explanation about the crime(s), detailing the crime(s) you were convicted of, the circumstances surrounding the crime(s), your age at the time you committed the crime, what punishment and/or restitution you completed, and what actions you have taken towards rehabilitation. It is our duty to inform you that your admission to and completion of massage school is not a guarantee that you will receive a license. The State Massage Board has the statutory authority to deny a license to anyone convicted of a felony and/or anyone found to be deficient in moral character. Your signature indicates that you attest that everything on this application is true and that you understand that The School is not making any claims that you are guaranteed to receive a massage license.

Signature_____**Date**_____

Form 2. Accompanying Documentation Checklist.

The following documentation must be attached to your application for admission to massage school. Applications with incomplete documentation will not be considered.

☐ Signed Student Enrollment Agreement

☐ Copy of your driver's license or passport

☐ Copy of your Social Security card

☐ Copy of your student liability insurance verification

☐ Copy of your high school diploma or college diploma

☐ Copy of any other professional licenses you hold

☐ Copy of transcript from previous massage school

☐ Copy of your Financial Aid contract

☐ Copy of your criminal record report

☐ Other_____

Form 3. Application Deficiency Form.

Dear_____,

Your application for admission to massage school is missing the following documentation. We cannot consider your application until all documents have been submitted to the school administrator. Your application will be kept on file for a period of 90 days, and if documentation has not been submitted within that time, you will need to reapply.

☐ Signed Student Enrollment Agreement

☐ Copy of your driver's license or other official state identification

☐ Copy of your Social Security card

☐ Copy of your student liability insurance verification

☐ Copy of your high school diploma or college diploma

☐ Copy of any other professional licenses you hold

☐ Copy of transcript from previous massage school

☐ Copy of your Financial Aid contract

☐ Copy of your criminal record report

☐ Other_____

Form 4. Student Enrollment Agreement.

This constitutes a contract between _____,

hereafter referred to as the School, and_____,

student (name)_____.

Student's address:_____

Phone #:_____e-mail_____

Social Security # _____

☐ I, _____hereby acknowledge that I

am enrolling as a student in the School.

☐ I understand that I am enrolling in a program that is _____

hours in length, and that my classes will commence on _____

and that I should expect to graduate on or about _____, providing

that I have met all the requirements for graduation.

☐ I understand that I am enrolling in the _____day or _____night

program, and that the days that I am expected to attend school are

_____ between the hours of_____.

☐ I understand that the tuition cost is _____, and that

I am ultimately responsible for payment of all tuition regardless of the

student loans or financial aid I may qualify for or receive, and that I

will not receive my final transcript and/or diploma until all monies

owed to The School are paid.

☐ I understand that this does not include the non-refundable application fee of _____, which is to be submitted along with my application to The School.

☐ I understand that additional costs over and above the tuition include _____ for textbooks, itemized list attached.

☐ I understand that I may purchase my textbooks on my own from another vendor and that I am obligated to purchase the edition currently on the itemized list provided by The School.

☐ I understand that I am obligated to purchase a massage table before attending the _____class meeting.

☐ I understand that I am also obligated to purchase the following school supplies at my own expense: three-ring binder, hole puncher, legal pads for note-taking, pens and pencils, a box of colored pencils, and unlined paper for drawing assignments.

☐ I understand that I am also obligated to purchase _____sets of twin/massage table sheets for use during clinical practice, including pillowcases for each set.

☐ I understand that I am obligated to purchase my own massage creams and oils.

☐ I understand that the school accepts cash, checks, money orders and _____credit cards.

☐ I understand that The School accepts financial aid, and that if I am applying for financial aid, I am obligated to meet with The School's financial officer at least one month prior to the beginning of school and at the end of every quarter.

☐ I understand that in the event I have a check returned for non-sufficient funds, that I will be charged a fee of _____.

☐ I understand that in the event I have two or more checks returned for non-sufficient funds, that I will be placed on a cash only basis with the school.

☐ I understand that if my tuition is not kept current, that I may be charged a late fee of _____ and interest of _____ monthly.

☐ I understand that any violation of the Code of Ethics of the Standards of Practice of the The School and/or licensing or accrediting bodies is grounds for dismissal from this school.

☐ I understand that I will not be entitled to any refund whatsoever if I am dismissed from this school for disciplinary reasons.

☐ I understand that policies that are not covered by this agreement are covered in the School Catalog and/or the Student Handbook and that I am obligated to read both in their entirety as soon as I am accepted as a student.

☐ I understand that I am responsible for obtaining student liability insurance within _____ days of my acceptance at The School.

☐ I understand that while I am a student of The School, I am representative of the school, and that being convicted of any violent or sexual offense will mean immediate dismissal from the school with no refund due.

☐ I understand that while The School maintains a list of facilities that are seeking massage therapists, they are in no way responsible for my employment or lack thereof after graduation.

☐ I understand that I have 72 hours after the signing of this contract to cancel it and receive a full refund, minus the non-refundable application fee of _____. I understand that if I decide to cancel this agreement after 72 hours of signing, that I will receive a refund in the amount of _____ if I drop out after the _____ class;

_____ if I drop out after the _____ class, and _____ if I decide to withdraw within _____ of the first date of class.

☐ I understand that if I decide to withdraw after _____ classes, I will not be entitled to any refund whatsoever, because at that point it will be too late to allow another student to take my place.

☐ By my signature, I hereby certify that I have read and understand the Student Enrollment Agreement, and that I agree to abide by all policies and procedures of The School.

Student's Signature_____Date_____

School Official's Signature_____Date_____

Form 5. Weekly Attendance Record.

Class_____**Instructor**_____
Week beginning_____

Student's Name	M	T	W	T	F	S	S

Form 6. Student Make-up Form.

Student_____Date_____

Dear_____,

You have missed the following class(es)_____
_____
_____

☐ You are obligated to make up this absence by attending class on _____or by making private arrangements for make-up with Instructor_____.

☐ Note that private make-ups are not covered by your tuition and you must pay the instructor directly at the time of the make-up.

☐ You are not obligated to attend a make-up class, but you are responsible   for obtaining all class notes and handouts and completing all class assignments.

☐ You are obligated to schedule a meeting with the Director immediately to discuss your excessive absences from class.

☐ You are obligated to meet with your Externship Supervisor at their convenience to arrange a make-up of your supervised clinical practice.

Instructor's Signature_____

Student's Signature _____
(student should sign to acknowledge receipt and return to instructor)

Form 7. Contractual Agreement for Student Externship.

This document represents a contract between
_____, hereafter referred to
as the School, and

_____, hereafter referred to
as the Facility.

☐ The Facility agrees that _____, a

student at the School, will be at their Facility for the purpose

of receiving clinical supervision in the practice of massage

therapy and bodywork.

☐ The Facility agrees that this is purely a voluntary agreement,

and that no payment of any kind will be received from the

school or the student in exchange for this supervision.

☐ The Facility acknowledges that while it is permissible for the

Facility to collect a fee for student services that no

compensation of any kind will be given to the student but

should be retained by the Facility.

☐ The Facility agrees to always acknowledge to clients that a

student will be performing their work or observing while a

professional representative of the Facility performs work.

☐ The Facility's representative agrees to sign the student's

documentation at the end of the work period.

☐ The Facility agrees that professional licensees are to provide direct clinical supervision, and promise to provide feedback to the student in a manner that is courteous, direct, and professional.

☐ The Facility acknowledges that any problems pertaining to the student or their work there will immediately be brought to the attention of the School Director.

☐ The Facility agrees that this agreement may be terminated in writing at any time by the school or by the representative of this Facility.

Signature of School Director_____Date_____

Signature of Facility Agent_____Date_____

Form 8. Client Documentation Form for Student Externship.

Student's Name_____

Externship
Facility_____Date_____

☐ By my signature below, I hereby acknowledge that I am receiving massage from a student from _____, a school of massage and bodywork.

☐ I understand that the student is receiving supervision credit for the work they perform at this facility.

☐ I understand that if any money is charged for this bodywork, that it is to be paid directly to the facility.

☐ I understand that students are prohibited from receiving compensation of any kind, including gratuities.

☐ I give my permission for this student to view my intake form and previous treatment notes while at this facility and understand that my confidential information will not be shared with anyone.

☐ I agree to offer feedback to the student before, during and/or after the massage, and will let them know if I want an adjustment in pressure, draping, avoidance of any parts of my body, or any other aspects of the session.

☐ I agree to inform the student of any health concerns I may have and medications that I am taking.

Please sign your name for documentation purposes for the student who is working with you today:

_____

Externship
Supervisor_____

Form 9. Student Community Service.

To be filled out by supervisor of community service event:

Student's Name_____

Event_____Date_____

The student identified him/herself to us upon arrival: Y   N

The student conducted him/herself in a professional manner: Y   N

The student had good personal hygiene and was dressed in clean, non-suggestive clothing: Y   N

The participants seemed pleased with the job the student did: Y   N

We would be glad to have this student at future events: Y   N

Coordinator's Signature_____

Student's Signature_____

Form 10. Intake Form for Student Clinic

Name_____Date_____

Address_____City_____ST_____Zip_____

Home Phone_____Cell/Work_____

Emergency
Contact_____Phone_____

Please answer the following questions for us so that your session may be conducted with safety and the most benefit to you:

1. Have you ever received a professional massage before?   Y   N

2. Are you pregnant?   Y   N

3. Are you suffering from any communicable diseases?   Y   N

4. Do you suffer from any of the following conditions? Please circle.

   Bruise easily   Neuropathy   Diabetes   Blood clots   Cancer
   Skin conditions (shingles, eczema, psoriasis, etc.) Seizures
   Any open cuts or wounds

5. Are you currently under a physician's care?   Y   N

6. Do you suffer from any repetitive motion or stress injuries such as Carpal Tunnel Syndrome, TMJ, or other such conditions? Y   N

7. Are there any areas of the body that you would like for us to avoid?

8. What do you hope to gain from today's session?

9. Are there any areas in particular that you have pain or tension in that you would like for us to focus on?

10.   Are you currently taking blood thinners, painkillers, muscle relaxants, or anti-inflammatory drugs? Y   N

I hereby acknowledge that I am aware that I am receiving bodywork from a student who is not licensed and is acting under supervision of school personnel. I understand that the intention of this bodywork is to help relieve stress and no is not a substitute for medical treatment and should not be construed as such. I understand massage therapists are not allowed to prescribe or diagnose.

Client Signature_____

Clinic Supervisor Signature_____

Form 11. Client Evaluation Form for Student Clinic.

Your feedback is important to the education of our students. Please give your evaluation to the supervisor on duty before leaving the clinic. This is an anonymous form, but if you have a complaint that should be addressed, please provide your name and contact information to the supervisor. We appreciate your honest and candid answers.

Name of Massage Student:_____

1. Did the therapist introduce himself/herself and call you by your name? Y N

2. Did the therapist explain where to put your clothes and jewelry, whether they would be starting the treatment face up or face down on the table, whether you should be under the cover, and answer any questions you have? Y N

3. Did the therapist ask if you needed to use the restroom or have a drink of water before the session? Y N

4. Did the therapist ask if there were any areas you did not want massaged? Y N

5. Did the therapist touch any areas that you had asked them to avoid? Y

6. Did the therapist explain the areas he/she was going to massage? Y N

7. Did the therapist ask you if you wanted a bolster under your knees when you were face up and under your ankles when you were face down? Y N

8. Were you comfortable during the treatment: Most of the time____ Some of the time____ All of the time____

9. Did the therapist go over the health intake form with you and conduct an interview prior to the session? Y N

10. Did the therapist have body odor or any odor of perfume/cologne? Y N

11. Did the therapist talk too much? Y N

12. Could you feel finger nails? Y N

13. Did the therapist keep his or her hands on you: All of the time____ Most of the time____ Some of the time____

14. Did the techniques seem: Too Slow____ Too Fast____ Just right____

15. Did the massage seem to have a smooth flow? Most of the time____ Some of the time____ None of the time____

16. Did the therapist seem confident? Y N

17. Did the therapist have gum or candy in their mouth? Y N

18. Did the therapist ever talk about sex, religion, race, or any other things that are inappropriate or that made you uncomfortable? Y N

19. How would you rate this therapist's personality and demeanor for dealing with the public? (1-10, 10 being the best). _____

20. In general, evaluate the effectiveness of the massage (1-10, 10 being the best). _____

21. Did the therapist spend too much or not enough time on any certain area? Y N

22. Did the therapist ask your preference on the amount of pressure before the massage, and check in with you during the massage? Y N

22. Would you make an appointment with this therapist when he/she graduates and becomes a professional therapist? Y N

23. What did you like best about the massage?_____

    _____

24. Do you have any suggestions for improvement for this therapist?_____

    _____

25. Did the therapist explain the possible side-effects from receiving a massage, such as soreness the next day, dizziness when getting up, flu-like symptoms, or any other possible issues?

26. Did the therapist offer you water after the massage? Y N

27. Did the therapist explain the benefits of receiving massage and encourage you to seek massage therapy again in the future? Y N

29. Any other comments you would care to make?

    _____
    _____
    _____

Form 12. Student Clinic Sign-in Form.

Please sign your name. You will be placed with your student massage therapist shortly. Thank you for patronizing our Student Clinic. We appreciate this opportunity to serve you.

CLIENT PLEASE SIGN-IN	APPOINMENT TIME	ASSIGNED STUDENT'S NAME

I hereby certify that this is an accurate record of the clients that received massage in the Student Clinic on_____(date).

Signature of Clinic
Supervisor_____

Form 13. Student SOAP Notes.

Client's Name_____Date_____

S:_____
_____
_____
O:_____
_____
A:_____
_____
P:_____
_____
_____

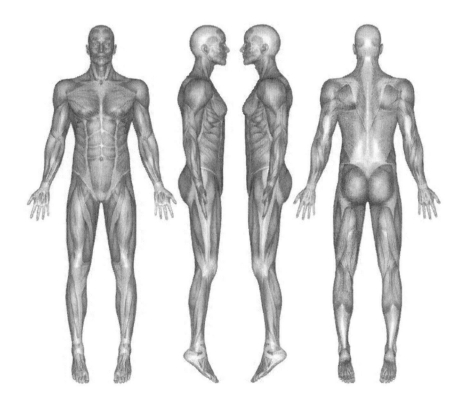

This client was seen at (check one):
☐ School Clinic
☐ School-Approved Externship Facility
☐ Community Service Event or other Fieldwork
☐ Client's home
☐ Student's home
☐ Other _____

Form 14. Job Description: School Director.

The School Director has ultimate responsibility for all operations of _____, hereafter referred to as the School. The School Director is responsible for delegating tasks to other staff members and faculty, and is responsible for ensuring all tasks that are delegated to others are accomplished. The School Director shall have the following qualifications:

- ☐ Possess a minimum of a _____ degree.
- ☐ Have a minimum of _____ years of professional experience in the field of massage and bodywork therapy.
- ☐ Have a minimum of _____ years experience as a lead instructor in one or more of the core curriculum courses that are presented in the school's curriculum.
- ☐ Have a minimum of _____ years experience in education administration.

At the discretion of the owner, the School Director may possess alternative qualifications that are equivalent to the requirements as described

An applicant for the position of School Director must submit the following:

- ☐ Copies of all academic diplomas or degrees
- ☐ Official school transcripts from all post-secondary institutions
- ☐ Copies of occupational licenses and certifications
- ☐ A detailed resume
- ☐ A record of training in teaching methods or history of previous teaching experience in a post-secondary institution
- ☐ A criminal record report
- ☐ Three letters of reference (not from relatives or former employers)

The School Director will personally be responsible for:

- ☐ Creation, and implementation of, all Policies and Procedures pertaining to The School.
- ☐ Interviewing, hiring, and firing of all staff members, including faculty and other support staff.
- ☐ Any disciplinary measures directed toward faculty, staff, or students as necessary.
- ☐ Conducting faculty and staff training, and performance reviews, on an ongoing basis.
- ☐ Supervision of maintenance of The School, including scheduling all cleaning, repairs as necessary, obtaining necessary inspections from the fire and health departments, and all other duties required to maintain a safe and comfortable environment for students and staff.
- ☐ Creation and implementation of the curriculum of The School.
- ☐ Creation and implementation of the academic schedule of The School.
- ☐ Creation of the school catalog, student handbook, and other publications as required for the operation of The School.

- Creation and/or approval of all advertising for The School.
- Review of all applications for admittance to the school, and the final decision of whether or not to admit, although other faculty members may be consulted when The Director deems necessary.
- Review of any and all complaints and suggestions by instructors, support staff, and office staff regarding school operations.
- Review of any and all complaints from students, regarding any perceived wrong committed by an instructor, staff member, or other student.
- Compliance of The School with all policies and procedures of the licensing body and/or accreditation body, including but not limited to licensure issues, ethical issues, Standard of Practice issues, fiduciary responsibility, and any other as necessary.
- Monthly internal audit of all financial accounts that have been maintained by the CFO.
- Reviewing the quarterly tax returns and quarterly audit with the CPA.
- Maintaining all required liability insurance and/or required bonding for The School.

Any and all other responsibilities that have not been listed here, or as may occur in the future, when adequate notice has been given by the owner and/or Board of Directors of The School.

Form 15. Job Description: Administrator.

The School Administrator will act as administrative assistant to the School Director and may perform any tasks delegated to the position as the Director sees fit. The Administrator will report directly to the Director of The School.

The School Administrator is to have the following responsibilities:

- Answering the phone and screening calls for the Director.
- Checking daily e-mails and phone messages and responding as appropriate.
- Checking daily mail, passing on to appropriate staff member.
- Ordering office and janitorial supplies (purchase order to be approved first by the Director).
- Public relations and recruitment of potential students; being prepared to answer their questions on the phone, by e-mail, and/or in person, giving tours of the school, assisting them in whatever manner to fill out applications for admittance, etc. and directing to CFO for financial matters.
- Maintaining student files (exclusive of financial records, which are the CFO's responsibility, but copies should be kept in the student file where the administrator may access them); being certain that all necessary documentation is in the files, including the student application, copies of financial documents, driver's license, SS card, green card or Visa if student is a foreign national, a signed copy of the student enrollment agreement, copies of any correspondence between the student and The School or its officers, transcripts from other schools, proof of graduation from HS, college transcripts where applicable, copies of any scholarships, financial aid documents, attendance records, and transcript/progress records from The School.
- Ordering textbooks and/or retail books as directed by the Director, first obtaining a signed purchase order, and maintaining an inventory.
- Establish and maintain relationships with NCBTMB, AMTA, ABMP, AFMTE, COMTA and any other organizations that are of benefit to students; prior to each new class coming in, contact the organizations to request their free student packets.
- Handle sales and ordering of massage tables, crèmes, and other necessary supplies and retail items (with purchase order signed by the Director).
- Posting student grades in report cards (which are then signed by the Director).
- Copying as needed.
- Running school-related errands for the Director as needed.
- Acting as a liason between the director and students as needed.
- Typing correspondence for the Director or other officers as needed.
- Maintain records of school personnel.

Any other duties as may be assigned with adequate notice by the Director on an as-needed basis.

Form 16. Job Description: Chief Financial Officer

The Chief Financial Officer, hereafter referred to as the CFO, will have responsibility for all financial affairs of The School at the Director's discretion and will report directly to The Director. The CFO may, at the Director's discretion, have the authority to sign checks and to act as an agent of The School.

The primary duties of the CFO are:

- To collect tuition and fees from students, give receipts, and post student accounts.
- To maintain all financial accounts of The School.
- To make deposits regularly.
- To reconcile bank statements monthly.
- To conduct regular monthly internal audits with the Director of The School and to inform Director immediately of any financial difficulties which may arise.
- To prepare paychecks for faculty and staff members.
- To maintain all correspondence from bank or credit agencies concerning school finances.
- To prepare student refunds when approved by the Director.
- To pay bills incurred by the school on time and to keep the Director apprised of financial transactions that exceed _____(insert amount), and to scrutinize all bills for accuracy.
- To see that retail merchandise, tables, supplies, etc are handled through a system of purchase orders.
- To give copies of all student financial transactions to the administrator to be placed in the student's file.
- To prepare financial statements etc as necessary for the CPA on a quarterly basis in expectation of paying quarterly taxes and to assist CPA as necessary.
- To prepare end-of-year forms such as W-2s, 1099s etc for paid staff and faculty members and give copy to administrator to be placed in their file.
- To obtain necessary tax forms from employees at time of hire and give to administrator to place in their file, and update on an annual basis.
- To handle applications for student financial aid, including scholarships and student loans.
- To facilitate The School's participation in all available financial aid sources.

Any other duties pertaining to financial matters of The School at the Director's discretion

Form 17. Job Description: Lead Instructor.

Lead instructors are to have the following credentials:

Be licensed for at least _____years if teaching a hands-on modality.

If teaching a science-based class, the instructor will have a minimum of a baccalaureate degree from a regionally accredited post-secondary college or university, and have at least _____ credit hours of academic course work in the subject area they teach. Alternatively, the following may be employed as a lead instructor: a licensed physician, chiropractor, osteopath, registered nurse, nurse practitioner, or physical therapist.

Lead instructors are to be trained in teaching methods and be able to carry out the following responsibilities:

- [ ] Development and implementation of lesson plans.
- [ ] Possess competent presentation skills.
- [ ] Maintain proper dynamics of student/teacher relationships.
- [ ] Manage the classroom environment.
- [ ] Evaluate student performances impartially and maintain student grade and attendance reports and report any potential problems immediately to the Director.
- [ ] Accommodate students with special needs.
- [ ] Be knowledgeable about all school policies and procedures.
- [ ] Be available when requested by the Director for ongoing teacher training and in-services.
- [ ] Maintain the student/teacher ratio of no more than ____:1.
- [ ] Maintain student paperwork as necessary, documentation of student complaints or problems that may arise involving students.
- [ ] Meet regularly with the Director to discuss any needed changes or problems that may arise.
- [ ] Adhere strictly to The Code of Ethics and model such for students.
- [ ] Provide an informative, safe, and non-discriminatory classroom environment for students.

Any other duties as may be required with adequate notice by the Director of The School.

Form 18. Job Description: Teaching Assistant.

Teaching Assistants are to have the following qualifications: Assistants in courses related to the theory and practice of massage and bodywork therapy shall be licensed for a period of at least ____ year(s), and shall have a minimum of _____ training in the subject matter of the course.

Teaching Assistants in courses other than theory and practice shall have training in the subject area, in addition to offering proof of at least _____ credit hours of post-secondary education in the subject area taught.

Teaching assistants will be mentored by the lead instructor to build competent planning, student communication, and presentation skills.

Teaching Assistants shall have the following responsibilities:

- ☐ Maintain proper dynamics of student/teacher relationships.
- ☐ Assist lead instructor in managing the classroom environment.
- ☐ Assist lead instructor in evaluating student performances impartially and maintenance of student grade and attendance reports and reporting any potential problems immediately to the lead instructor.
- ☐ Accommodate students with special needs.
- ☐ Be knowledgeable about all school policies and procedures.
- ☐ Be available when requested by the Director and/or lead instructor for ongoing teacher training and in-services.
- ☐ Assist lead instructor in maintaining the student/teacher ratio of no more than _____:1.
- ☐ Assist lead instructor in maintaining student paperwork as necessary, documentation of student complaints or problems that may arise involving students.
- ☐ Meet regularly with the lead instructor, and Director if requested, to discuss any needed changes or problems that may arise.
- ☐ Adhere strictly to The Code of Ethics.
- ☐ Provide an informative, safe, and non-discriminatory classroom environment for students.

Any other duties as may be required with adequate notice by the lead instructor or the Director of The School.

Form 19. Job Description: Adjunct Instructor.

Instructors who provide no more than three hours of instruction in a program are exempt from the rules governing the qualifications of permanent instructors but are expected to abide by the following guidelines.

The functions and responsibilities of Adjunct Instructors are:

- ☐ Development and implementation of lesson plans in their subject area.
- ☐ Possess competent presentation skills.
- ☐ Maintain proper dynamics of student/teacher relationships.
- ☐ Manage the classroom environment.
- ☐ Evaluate student performances impartially and maintain student grade and attendance reports, reporting any potential problems immediately to the Director.
- ☐ Accommodate students with special needs.
- ☐ Be knowledgeable about all school policies and procedures.
- ☐ Be available when requested by the Director for ongoing teacher training and in-services.
- ☐ Maintain the student/teacher ratio of no more than 20:1.
- ☐ Maintain student paperwork as necessary, documentation of student complaints or problems that may arise involving students.
- ☐ Meet when required with the Director to discuss any curriculum changes or problems that may arise.
- ☐ Adhere strictly to The Code of Ethics .
- ☐ Provide an informative, safe, and non-discriminatory classroom environment for students.
- ☐ Any other duties as may be required by the Director of The School.

Form 20. Job Description: Externship Supervisor.

Externship Supervisors, hereafter referred to as the ES, shall be licensed for at least two years, except in the instances where the modality being supervised is exempt from the licensing requirements. The functions and responsibilities of the ES are:

- [ ] To provide supervised practicum opportunities for students.
- [ ] To provide guidance and feedback to the student, verbally and written when necessary.
- [ ] To document the completion of supervision hours as required by the Director.
- [ ] To communicate directly with the student regarding their requirements for supervision, such as days and hours of expected service, dress requirements, intake and SOAP note requirements in accordance with the rules of their own business.
- [ ] To maintain communication with the Director as needed.
- [ ] To immediately bring to the Director's attention any problems arising from student misconduct, violations of The Code of Ethics, or policies and procedures of The School.
- [ ] Externship Supervisors may be obligated to attend a yearly inservice in Externship Supervision held at the Director's discretion.

Form 21. Staff Contract.

This contract is to be considered a binding document between
_____, Employee,
and _____, referred to hereafter
as The School.

- ☐ I understand that I am being hired for the position of
  _____.
- ☐ I understand that my employment commences on the date
  of_____and that this contract expires
  effective_____.
- ☐ I understand that my duties are as outlined in the Job Description that I have
  been provided, and that I have read and acknowledge that I thoroughly
  understand said description prior to agreeing to this employment, including
  my obligation to attend inservice training as necessary.
- ☐ I understand that the payment I am receiving is at the rate of
  _____per_____ for the duration of this contract, and that any
  change in that rate prior to the expiration of this contract is strictly at the
  discretion of the Director of The School.
- ☐ I understand that the additional benefits of this employment are as listed
  below:
- ☐ I understand that that I am obligated to be at work on _____(days)
  between the hours of _____. I understand that this schedule may be
  subject to change with _____notice, and that if I am unable to fulfill my
  duties due to the change in schedule, that I may be released from my duties
  within such period of notice.
- ☐ I understand that I am to uphold all Policies and Procedures of The School,
  and that my failure to do so may result in immediate termination.
- ☐ I understand that I am obligated to uphold The Code of Ethics of the State
  Board of Massage & Bodywork Therapy, whether or not I am licensed as a
  therapist myself, and that failure to do so is cause for immediate termination.
- ☐ I understand that this job requires that I deal with existing students, potential
  students, and the public at large, and that I am required to perform my duties
  with tact and in a non-discriminatory way, and I agree to always represent
  The School in the best possible light in the performance of my duties.
- ☐ I understand that in the event of unsatisfactory performance, I may be given
  a verbal warning, a written warning, or placed on employment probation by
  the Director of The School.
- ☐ I understand that any failure to carry out my duties as outlined in this
  contract is cause for termination without further benefit or obligation on the
  part of The School.
- ☐ I understand that The School is to be in possession of the following
  documents and that they are to remain in my personnel file even in the event
  of my termination:

_____Copy of my employment application

_____Copy of my criminal record report
_____Copy of all academic diplomas or degrees
_____Official school transcripts from all post-secondary institutions
_____A record of work experience in the field
_____A record of training in teaching methods if applicable to my position
_____A copy of my driver's license
_____A copy of my Social Security card
_____A copy of occupational licenses and certifications
_____A copy of a signed release form from a physician stating that I am free of
     communicable diseases or other conditions that would prevent my carrying
     out my duties

Employee's signature_____Date_____

Director's signature_____Date_____

Form 22. Staff Evaluation.

Evaluation for staff member_____Date_____

Position of staff member_____

Area of Evaluation	Satisfactory	Unsatisfactory	Needs Improvement
Performs duties as outlined on job description			
Adheres to work schedule, is on time, no excessive absences or tardiness			
Meets deadlines for assigned work			
Works well with other members of the team			
Models ethical and professional behavior in all activities			
Attends required inservice training			

Problems noted:

Actions to be taken:

Acknowledgement of evaluation:

I, _____, acknowledge that I have been evaluated, my job performance discussed, and informed of any actions to be taken on my part and/or the part of management.

Signature of staff member_____

Signature of owner/evaluator_____

Form 23. Student Class Evaluation.

Please rate the presentation, design, and value of this class. Do not write your name on this paper. This is an anonymous evaluation. We will consider your reactions and suggestions in planning future classes.

CLASS:_____ Date: _____

INSTRUCTOR(s): _____

Please circle the answer which best describes your reaction to each of the following:

1. My expectations of this class were   exceeded   met   not met

2. The teacher's knowledge of the topic appeared to be
   excellent   better than average   about average   poor

3. The teacher's presentation was
   excellent   better than average   about average   poor

4. The physical and organization aspects of this class were
   excellent   better than average   about average   poor

5. Overall, I would say that my attendance at this class should prove   beneficial
   not beneficial

6. The most beneficial features of this class were
   _____

7. What suggestions would you give to improve this class?
   _____

8. What changes do you plan to make in your work as a result of this
   class?_____

9. Would you recommend this class to other students? Yes   No

   Any other comments:

Form 24. Summary of Class Evaluations

Class_____Date_____

Instructor(s)_____

For your information and your benefit as you plan future classes, here is a summary of the student evaluations from your recent class.

% of students who said their expectations of this class were

Exceeded_____   Met_____   Not Met_____

The table below reflects the percentage of students who said:

	Excellent	Better than average	Average	Poor
Teacher's knowledge of the topic				
Teacher's presentation skills				
Physical and organizational aspects of the class				

% of students who said attending the class was beneficial: Yes_____ No_____

% of students who said they would recommend this class: Yes_____ No_____

Compliments:

Suggestions for improvement:

Please sign below to acknowledge that you have read this summary and return to the Director.

Instructor's Signature_____

Form 25. Student Report Card.

Student_____ID_____

SUBJECT	1st Q	2nd Q	3rd Q	4th Q
Theory & Practice of Massage & Bodywork				
Anatomy and Physiology				
Pathology				
Kinesiology				
Business and Marketing				
Professional Ethics				
Neuromuscular Therapy				
Hydrotherapy				
Medical Terminology				
Holistic Healing Modalities				
Supervised Student Clinic				
Self-Care for the Therapist				
Community Service Projects				
Externship				
Graduation Projec				
Total Number of Credit Hours				

Signature of Director_____Date_____

Form 26. Official Student Transcript.

Student_____ID#_____

SUBJECT	Total Hours	Grade
Theory & Practice of Massage & Bodywork		
Anatomy and Physiology		
Pathology		
Kinesiology		
Business and Marketing		
Professional Ethics		
Neuromuscular Therapy		
Hydrotherapy		
Medical Terminology		
Holistic Healing Modalities		
Supervised Student Clinic		
Self-Care for the Therapist		
Community Service Projects		
Externship		
Graduation Project		
Total Number of Credit Hours		

Signature of Director_____**Date**_____

Form 27. Permission to Release Student Records.

I, _____, hereby authorize The School
to release my student records, including but not limited to my report card and final
transcript to

☐ _____(Name of Institution or Employer)

☐ _____(Name of Institution or Employer)

☐ _____(Name of Institution or Employer)

☐ Any school or employer who requests the information

I understand that I may revoke this permission by notifying the school in writing.

Signed_____Date_____

Witness_____ Date_____

Appendix II

State Massage Therapy Boards

State of Alabama
Board of Massage Therapy
2777 Zelda Road
Montgomery, AL 36106
334/269-9990 or
866-873-4664
334/263-6115 (fax)
massagetherapy@warrenandco.com

Alaska is currently an unregulated state.

State of Arizona
Board of Massage Therapy
1400 West Washington, Suite# 300
Phoenix, Arizona 85007
(602) 542-8604
www.massageboard.az.gov

Arkansas State Board of Massage Therapy
101 East Capitol Avenue Suite 460
P.O. Box 2019
Little Rock, Arkansas 72201 (501)
683-1448
www.arkansasmassagetherapy.com

California Massage Therapy Council
One Capitol Mall, Suite 320
Sacramento, CA 95814
Phone: (916) 669-5336
www.camtc.org

Colorado Department of Regulatory Boards
Massage Therapist Registration
1560 Broadway
Suite 1550
Denver, CO 80202 (303) 894-7855
www.dora.state.co.us/massage-therapists

Connecticut Department of Public Health
Massage Therapist Licensure
410 Capitol Ave., MS # 12 APP
P.O. Box 340308
Hartford, CT 06134
860-509-8000
http://www.ct.gov/dph

State of Delaware
Board of Massage & Bodywork
Cannon Building,
Suite 203
861 Silver Lake Blvd.
Dover, DE 19904
(302) 744-4500
http://dpr.delaware.gov/boards/massagebodyworks

Florida Department of Health
Board of Massage Therapy
4052 Bald Cypress Way
Bin C-06
Tallahassee, FL 32399
850-245-4161
www.doh.state.fl.us/mqa/massage

Georgia Board of Massage Therapy
237 Coliseum Drive
Macon, GA 31217-3858
(478) 207-2440
http://sos.georgia.gov/plb/massage/

Hawaii
DCCA-PVL
Att: Massage
P.O. Box 3469
Honolulu, HI 96801 (808) 586-2694
http://hawaii.gov/dcca/pvl/boards/massage

Idaho is currently an unregulated state.

Illinois Department of Financial & Professional Regulation
Massage Therapy Licensure
320 W Washington Street, Fl 3
Springfield, IL 62786
Phone:217-782-8556
http://www.idfpr.com/profs/info/MassageTherapy.asp

Chicago office:

100 West Randolph, 9th Floor
Chicago, Illinois 60601
Phone: 312-814-4500

State of Indiana
Professional Licensing Agency
Attn: State Board of Massage Therapy
402 W Washington St, Room W072
Indianapolis, Indiana 46204
Staff Phone Number: 317-234-2051
http://www.in.gov/pla/massage.htm

Iowa Board of Massage Therapy
Lucas State Ofc. Bldg.
321 E. 12th Street
Des Moines, IA 50319 (515) 281-6959
http://www.idph.state.ia.us/licensure/board_home.asp?board=mt

Kentucky Board of Massage Therapy
911 Leawood Drive
Frankfort, KY 40601
502-564-3296, ext. 239
http://bmt.ky.gov/Pages/default.aspx

Louisiana Board of Massage Therapy
12022 Plank Road
Baton Rouge, LA 70811
(225) 771-4090
www.labmt.org

State of Maine
Office of Professional and Occupational Regulation
Attn: Massage Therapy
35 State House Station
Augusta, Maine 04333-0035
207-624-8603
http://www.maine.gov/pfr/professionallicensing/contact_us.htm

Maryland Board of Chiropractic and Massage Therapy Examiners
4201 Patterson Avenue
Baltimore, Maryland 21215
410-764-4738
http://dhmh.md.gov/massage

Massachusetts Board of Registration of Massage Therapy
1000 Washington Street, Suite 710
Boston, Massachusetts 02118 (617) 727-
3074 www.mass.gov/ocabr/licensee/dpl-
boards/mt

Michigan Board of Massage Therapy
You can send an e-mail to bhpinfo@michigan.gov for information. According to their general government website as of 07/12/2012, they expect to start the licensing process in the fall of 2012.

Minnesota is currently an unregulated state.

Mississippi State Board of Massage Therapy
PO Box 20
Morton, MS 39117
Phone: 601-732-6038
http://www.msbmt.state.ms.us/msbmt/web.nsf

Missouri Board of Therapeutic Massage
3605 Missouri Boulevard
P.O. Box 1335
Jefferson City, MO 65102-1335
573-522-6277
http://pr.mo.gov/massage.asp

Montana Board of Massage Therapy
301 South Park , 4th Floor
P.O. Box 200513
Helena, MT 59620-0513 (406) 841-2037
http://bsd.dli.mt.gov/license/bsd_boards/lmt_board/board_page.asp

Nebraska Department of Health & Human Services
Massage Therapy
301 Centennial Mall South, Lincoln, Nebraska 68509 (402) 471-3121
http://dhhs.ne.gov/publichealth/Pages/crl_mhcs_mass_massage.aspx

Nevada Board of Massage Therapists
1755 E. Plumb Lane Suite 252
Reno, NV 89502 (775) 688-
1888
http://massagetherapy.nv.gov/

Licensing and Regulative Services
Office of Operations Support
New Hampshire Department of Health and Human Services
129 Pleasant Street
Concord, New Hampshire 03301 (603) 271-0853
http://www.nh.gov/nhes/elmi/licertoccs/massage.htm

Massage, Bodywork & Therapy Committee
New Jersey Board of Nursing
PO Box 45010
Newark, NJ 07101 (973) 504-6430
http://www.nj.gov/lps/ca/massage/

New Mexico Massage Therapy Board
Toney Anaya Building, Second Floor
2550 Cerrillos Road
Santa Fe, NM 87505
(505) 476-4870
http://www.rld.state.nm.us/Massage/index.html

State of New York
Massage Therapy
Office of the Professions State Education Building – 2nd Floor
Albany, NY 12234
518-474-3817
http://www.op.nysed.gov/prof/mt/

North Carolina Board of Massage & Bodywork Therapy
Post Office Box 2539
Raleigh, NC 27602
919-546-0050
www.bmbt.org

North Dakota Board of Massage
POB 218
Beach, ND 58621
701-872-4895
www.ndboardofmassage.com

Ohio Medical Board
Massage Therapy
30 East Broad Street, 3rd Floor
Columbus, Ohio 43215-6127
(614) 466-3934
http://www.med.ohio.gov/mt_about_massage_therapy.htm

Oklahoma is currently an unregulated state.

Oregon Board of Massage Therapists
748 Hawthorne Avenue NE
Salem, OR 97301
503-365-8657
http://www.oregon.gov/OBMT/

Pennsylvania State Board of Massage Therapy
P.O. Box 2649, Harrisburg, PA 17105-2649
(717) 783-7155
http://www.portal.state.pa.us/portal/server.pt/community/state_board_of_massage_therapy/12529

Rhode Island Board of Massage Therapy
Room 104
3 Capitol Hill
Providence, Rhode Island 02908
401-222-2828
http://www.health.ri.gov/licenses/healthcare/index.php

South Carolina Board of Massage & Bodywork Therapy
PO Box 11329
Columbia, S.C. 29211-1329 (803) 896-4588
http://www.llr.state.sc.us/POL/MassageTherapy/

South Dakota Board of Massage Therapy
POB 1062
Sioux Falls, SD 57101-1062
605-271-7103
http://doh.sd.gov/boards/massage/

Tennessee Board of Massage Licensure
227 French Landing, Suite 300
Nashville, TN 37243
800-778-4123
http://health.state.tn.us/boards/massage/

Texas Department of State Health Services
Massage Therapy Licensing Program
Mail Code 1982
P.O. Box 149347
Austin , Texas 78714 (512) 834-6616
http://www.dshs.state.tx.us/massage/

Utah Division of Occupational & Professional Licensing
Massage Therapy
160 East 300 South
Salt Lake City, Utah 84111 (801) 530-6628
http://www.dopl.utah.gov/licensing/massage_therapy.html

Virginia Board of Nursing
Massage Therapy Division
Perimeter Center
9960 Mayland Drive, Suite 300
Henrico, Virginia 23233-1463
(804) 367-4400
http://www.dhp.virginia.gov

Washington DC Department of Health
Board of Massage Therapy
899 North Capitol Street, NE
First Floor
Washington, DC 20002 (877) 672-2174
http://hpla.doh.dc.gov/hpla/cwp/view,A,1195,Q,488659,hplaNav,|30661|,.asp

Washington State Department of Health
Health Professions & Facilities
Massage Therapy
243 & 310 Israel Rd SE
P.O. Box 47865
Olympia, Washington, 98504-7865
http://www.doh.wa.gov/hsqa/professions/Massage_Therapy/default.htm

West Virginia Massage Therapy Licensure
179 Summers Street
Suite 711
Charleston, WV 25301 Phone:
304-558-1060
www.wvmassage.org

Wisconsin Massage Therapy & Bodywork Therapy Affiliated Credentialing Board
State of Wisconsin Dept. of Safety and Professional Services
PO Box 8935
Madison, WI 53708-8935
(877)617-1565

dwl.wi.gov

Appendix III
Massage Therapy Organizations

Alliance for Massage Therapy Education
1760 Old Meadow Road, Suite 500
McLean, Virginia 22102
1- 855-236-8331
www.afmte.org

American Massage Therapy Association
500 Davis Street
Evanston, Il 60201
1-877-905-0577
www.amtamassage.org

Associated Bodywork & Massage Professionals
25188 Genesee Trail Road
Golden, CO 80401
800-458-2267
www.abmp.com

Commission on Massage Therapy Accreditation
5335 Wisconsin Avenue, NW, Suite 440
Washington, D.C. 20015
202-895-1518
www.comta.org

Federation of State Massage Therapy Boards
7111 W. 51st Street, Suite 356
Overland Park, Kansas 66223
913-681-0380
www.fsmtb.org

Massage Therapy Foundation
500 Davis Street, Suite 900
Evanston, IL 60201
847-869-5019
www.massagetherapyfoundation.org

National Certification Board for Therapeutic Massage & Bodywork
1901 S. Meyers Rd., Suite 240
Oakbrook Terrace, IL 60181-5243
1-800-296-0664
www.ncbtmb.org

Appendix IV

Research Resources

American Massage Therapy Association	http://www.amtamassage.org/infocenter/research_scientific-and-medical-research.html
International Journal of Therapeutic Massage & Bodywork	http://www.ijtmb.org/index.php/ijtmb
Massage Therapist's Association of British Columbia	https://www.massagetherapy.bc.ca/why-join/research
Massage Therapy Foundation	http://www.massagetherapyfoundation.org
Massage Therapy Research Consortium	http://www.massagetherapyresearchconsortium.com/
National Center for Complimentary & Alternative Medicine	http://nccam.nih.gov/health/massage/
Orthopedic Massage Education & Research Institute	http://www.omeri.com/
PubMed	http://www.ncbi.nlm.nih.gov/pubmed/
Touch Research Institute	http://www6.miami.edu/touch-research/

Appendix V

Teacher Training

A complete listing of teacher training offered by instructors who are Approved Providers under the National Certification Board for Therapeutic Massage & Bodywork may be found on their website at www.ncbtmb.org The providers listed here are those that we know personally, have taken a class or workshop from, or heard as keynote speakers at education conferences.

Judith Aston	http://www.astonkinetics.com
Keith Bouchard	http://www.healingartsschool.com
Sharon Burch	http://www.homestudycredits.org
Scott Dartnall	http://www.worldmassageconference.com
Sandy Fritz	http://www.healthenrichment.com
Brian Halterman	http://www.abmp.com
Shelley Johnson	http://www.kneadedenergy.com
Monica Love	http://www.amtamassage.org
Rick Rosen	http://www.massage.net
Carey Smith	http://www.massage.net
Jan Schwartz & Whitney Lowe	http://www.educationtrainingsolutions.com
Cherie Sohnen-Moe	http://www.sohnen-moe.com
Diana L. Thompson	http://www.handsheal.com
Ariana Vincent	http://www.arianainstitute.com
Nancy Toner Weinberger	http://www.dynamicequilibrium.com
Ruth Werner	http://www.ruthwerner.com
Anne Williams	http://www.LWW.com

Index

$1.00 from the sale of each copy of this book will be donated to the Alliance for Massage Therapy Education.

Please donate to the Alliance for Massage Therapy Education by visiting their website at **www.afmte.org**

We encourage everyone involved in massage therapy education and all related industry partners to join the Alliance.

Thank you for your support!

Made in the USA
Lexington, KY
14 September 2012